A Guide to East Asian Collections in North America

A Guide to East Asian Collections in North America

Compiled by

Thomas H. Lee

Bibliographies and Indexes in World History, Number 25

Greenwood Press
New York • Westport, Connecticut • London

Library of Congress Cataloging-in-Publication Data

Lee, Thomas H.
   A guide to East Asian collections in North America / compiled by
Thomas H. Lee.
     p. cm.—(Bibliographies and indexes in world history, ISSN
0742-6852 ; no. 25)
   Includes bibliographies and index.
   ISBN 0-313-27397-9
   1. East Asia—Library resources. 2. Library resources—North
America—Bibliography. I. Title. II. Series.
Z3001.L4 1992
[DS504.5]
016.95—dc20   91-46698

British Library Cataloguing in Publication Data is available.

Library of Congress Catalog Card Number: 91-46698
ISBN: 0-313-27397-9
ISSN: 0742-6852

First published in 1992

Greenwood Press, 88 Post Road West, Westport, CT 06881
An imprint of Greenwood Publishing Group, Inc.

Printed in the United States of America

∞™

The paper used in this book complies with the
Permanent Paper Standard issued by the National
Information Standards Organization (Z39.48-1984).

10 9 8 7 6 5 4 3 2 1

To

Yvonne, Amy, and Michelle

Contents

Preface

The aim of this guide is to introduce the major East Asian collections in North America to scholars and researchers engaged in East Asian studies. In spite of the vast and daily growing East Asian resources in American libraries, a comprehensive guide, one that is specifically designed for East Asian collections and provides more detailed information about them than can be found in the general listings of libraries, has until now been lacking. The present volume has been compiled to fill this gap.

East Asian language materials entered American libraries early. In 1869, the first batch of such materials, 933 Chinese volumes in 130 *t'ao* (or cases), reached North America as gifts from the Ch'ing Emperor to the United States government.[1] These books, now kept in the Chinese rare book collection of the Library of Congress, marked the beginning of the development of East Asian collections in North America. Since 1869, East Asian materials have continued to arrive in American libraries. During the past hundred years or so, the growth of East Asian materials and the increase of the numbers of East Asian collections in North America have been steady and at times, phenomenal. Some milestone surveys done in recent decades by the Committee on East Asian Libraries (CEAL) of the Association for Asian Studies, the professional organization representing East Asian libraries in North America, indicate that by 1975, there were about 6.7 million volumes in 93 collections.[2]   In 1980, the number of volumes increased to about 7.9 million as reported by 92 collections.[3] Since 1989, CEAL has been conducting annual surveys of library resources among its members. The report on its latest survey, published in spring 1991, reveals that the current holdings of East Asian collections in North America, even with only the larger collections reporting, have exceeded 10 million volumes.[4]

This guide covers fifty-five major East Asian collections. Here a "major collection" is defined as one that has about 20,000 or more East Asian volumes in its holdings and an active, on-going collection development program.   These collections were selected from among those which participated in the most recent CEAL survey, plus a few others which did not respond to the CEAL survey but are nonetheless worthy of inclusion because of their substantial holdings. Of the fifty-five collections, fifty-two are located in the United States, and three in Canada. Together they house over 10 million volumes and about half a million microform items. These holdings represent the bulk of East Asian resources that are serving the needs of East Asian area studies in North America.

Descriptions of the collections are based on information gathered through a survey of the East Asian libraries conducted during the period between the fall of 1990 and spring of 1991.   A specially designed questionnaire was sent to the responsible librarians of these selected collections to obtain the types of information that would fit into all the categories to be covered by this guide. The responses to the survey by East Asian library colleagues were enthusiastic and complete, with a return rate of 100 percent. Many not only sent back the completed questionnaires, but also provided supplementary materials such as library handbooks, brochures, and other forms of publication that shed additional light on their collections and answered questions on direct contact by telephone or personal correspondence. Based on the information received, each of the collections in this guide is described in terms of contact, holdings, subject strengths, special materials and collections, access services, material processing and organization, network and consortium participation, and publications.

Scope and Arrangement

This guide focuses on East Asian collections in general research and public libraries. The few special libraries selected are for their extensive and more comprehensive holdings on East Asian subjects.   The guide deals primarily with materials in East Asian vernacular languages, mainly Chinese, Japanese, and Korean.   Some notable Tibetan, Manchu, and Mongolian collections are also mentioned as part of the descriptions of Chinese holdings reported by some larger collections. Materials in both book and nonbook format are covered.

Entries of collections are arranged alphabetically by the names of the parent institutions or, in the cases of the few independent East Asian libraries, by their own names. U.S. and Canadian libraries are listed in the same alphabetical sequence. Entries are also numbered according to their alphabetical order for easy reference. A list of the collections by geographical areas is appended at the end of the guide to give the readers a general idea of the spread and distribution of the East Asian resources in the whole region.

The index contains references to special collections, rare items, distinctive or variant names of libraries, names of individuals, and subjects. The subject terms refer to the more special and unique materials described in the entries. The readers are advised that all the collections included in this guide, except for the very few specialized ones, have a good and comprehensive coverage of the general subjects in East Asian humanities and social sciences, and are capable of providing them, to the extent supported by their holdings, with research materials in the general fields of East Asian studies.

Acknowledgements

I would like to give special thanks to all the East Asian library colleagues who have taken time out of their busy work schedules to respond to my questionnaires. Without their help and cooperation, the compilation of this guide would never have been possible. I wish to also thank the Library of Indiana University for giving me the research leave and grant to accomplish what I have set out to do with this book project. To my family, I owe a word of appreciation to my wife and colleague, Yvonne, and daughters, Amy and Michelle, for their advice and support during the compilation of this guide.

In presenting this guide to its potential users, I would welcome any comments or suggestions that may pave the way for future editions.

Notes

1. Tsuen-hsuin Tsien, "First Chinese-American Exchange of Publications," Harvard Journal of Asiatic Studies 25 (1964-1965): 19.

2. Tsuen-hsuin Tsien, Current Status of East Asian Collections in American Libraries, 1974/1975 (Washington, D.C.: Center for Chinese Research Materials, Association of Research Libraries, 1976), p. 2.

3. "Current Status of East Asian Collections in American Libraries: A Preliminary Report for 1979/80," <u>CEAL Bulletin</u> no. 67 (February 1982): 25.

4. "Current Status of East Asian Collections in American Libraries, 1989/1990," <u>CEAL Bulletin</u> no. 92 (February 1991): 33-34.

Explanatory Notes

Description of collections in this guide is given according to the following uniform outline:

Heading: Name of the institution and its East Asian library/collection with contact information.

Year: The year when a library was founded or a collection was started.

Hours: Hours when the library is open and the collection is accessible to the users. Many university libraries have varied open hours during summer, intersessions, and holidays. Readers are advised to check ahead when making visits during these periods.

Holdings: Holdings given are those reported as of June 30, 1990, unless indicated otherwise (a couple of the collections reported their holdings with a slightly later cut-off date and these are noted in the entries).

Areas of strength: General description of the collection in terms of collection emphases and subject strengths.

Special collections: Introduction to important holdings of special materials within the East Asian collection.

East Asian materials in other collections: East Asian materials held by libraries other than the East Asian collection on the same university campus.

Access: Policies and regulations of the library regarding in-house use and on-site borrowing of materials.

Travel grants: Some larger East Asian collections regularly offer travel support to out-of-town users. Information about regulations and application procedures is given where such support is available.

Interlibrary loan service: Availability of the service to other libraries. In general, most of the collections covered by this guide will lend out books (except reference books) and microfilms, but not periodicals and newspapers.

Online cataloging: The library's participation in either of the two national databases, OCLC or RLIN, for inputting its East Asian vernacular bibliographic records. Both OCLC and RLIN have a CJK sub-system which is capable of creating and displaying East Asian vernacular scripts in their bibliographic records.

Catalogs for use of the collection: Availability of card catalogs and/or online catalogs that can be used by the users for bibliographic searching of the library's holdings.

Network/Consortium affiliation: The library's participation in regional and/or national cooperative programs.

Publications: List of printed catalogs, checklists of holdings, and other publications that describe a library's collections.

Abbreviations

CEAL   Committee on East Asian Libraries, Association for Asian Studies

CIC   Committee on Institutional Cooperation (a regional cooperative program participated by the eleven universities in the Midwest: Chicago, Illinois, Iowa, Michigan, Michigan State, Minnesota, Northwestern, Ohio State, Purdue, and Wisconsin)

CJK   Chinese, Japanese, and Korean

CONSER   Cooperative Online Serials (a national cooperative system for cataloging serials supported by the Library of Congress)

OCLC   Online Computer Library Center (a national database with a CJK subsystem that can create, store, retrieve, and display CJK vernacular scripts for its bibliographic records)

RLG   Research Libraries Group

RLIN   Research Libraries Information Network of RLG (a national database with a CJK subsystem that can create, store, retrieve, and display CJK vernacular scripts for its bibliographic records)

UTLAS   UTLAS International, Canada (formerly University of Toronto Library Automation System)

Collections

(Alphabetically arranged by institutions)

1. UNIVERSITY OF ARIZONA

Oriental Studies Collection, University Library
Tucson, Arizona 85721
Tel: (602) 621-6380. FAX: (602) 621-4619

Ju-yen Teng, Head

Year started: 1964

Hours:

Weekdays: 7:00 am - Midnight
Saturday: 9:00 am - 6:00 pm
Sunday: 10:00 am - Midnight

Holdings:

Volumes:
Chinese:	107,923
Japanese:	33,756

Current serials:
Chinese:	250
Japanese:	250

Current newspapers:
Chinese:	9
Japanese:	3
East Asian microfilm reels and fiche cards:	900

Areas of strength:

Chinese and Japanese materials in the humanities and social sciences are collected. Emphases of the collection are:

Chinese: Pre-modern history (especially history of the Sung dynasty), pre-modern literature (especially literature of the T'ang dynasty), language, and Buddhism.

Japanese: Language and linguistics, modern history, Japanese studies on Chinese history and literature, and Buddhism.

Access:

The library is open to the public. Borrowing privileges are given to the following categories of users:

   a) University of Arizona faculty, students, and staff
   b) University of Arizona alumni (with library cards)
   c) Arizona state residents (with library cards)
   d) Faculty members of the Arizona State University and the Northern Arizona University
   e) Visiting scholars associated with the university

Interlibrary loan service:

Available to all libraries.

Online cataloging:

East Asian materials are cataloged in the OCLC CJK system.

Catalogs for use of the collection:

Card Catalogs: East Asian card catalogs are maintained.

Online Catalog: The local online catalog, GEAC, includes East Asian bibliographic records for author and title entries in romanization only.

Network/Consortium affiliation:

Member of OCLC.

2. ARIZONA STATE UNIVERSITY

East Asian Language Collection, University Libraries
Tempe, Arizona 85287-1006
Tel: (602) 965-7240. FAX: (602) 965-9169.

Ai-Hwa Wu, Chinese Studies Librarian
Kasuko Hotelling, Japanese Studies Librarian

Year started: 1973

Hours:

Monday-Thursday: 7:00 am - Midnight
Friday: 7:00 am - 9:00 pm
Saturday: 9:00 am - 8:00 pm.
Sunday: 10:00 am - Midnight

Holdings:

Total CJK volumes: 51,486. Current CJK serials and newspapers: 200.

Areas of strength:

East Asian materials in the humanities and social sciences are collected. Emphases of the collection are:

Chinese: Art history, history (especially the history of Sung and Ch'ing dynasties), language, literature, philosophy, and political science.

Japanese: Art history, Buddhism, history, language, literature, and political science.

Korean: History and political science.

Some special materials including art items and a rare rubbing of Wen Cheng-ming (1470-1559) are kept in the main library's Special (Rare) Collections.

Access:

The library is open to the public. It participates in the OCLC Reciprocal Faculty Borrowing Program which allows faculty members of participating institutions borrowing privileges and on-site access to collections of OCLC research libraries. The East Asian Collection also joins the shared resources program of RLG for CJK materials.

Interlibrary loan service:

Available to all libraries.

Online cataloging:

East Asian materials are cataloged in the RLIN CJK system.

Catalogs for use of the collection:

Card catalogs: East Asian card catalogs are maintained but closed since June 1988. A retrospective conversion of holdings in the card catalogs before 1989 is being planned.

Online catalog: The local online catalog, CARL (Colorado Alliance of Research Libraries), contains romanized records for recently acquired and processed East Asian materials that have been cataloged online in the RLIN database.

Network/Consortium affiliation:

Member of RLG and SOLAR (the Serials Online in Arizona).

3. BRIGHAM YOUNG UNIVERSITY

Asian Collection, Harold B. Lee Library, Provo, Utah 84602
Tel: (801) 378-4061. FAX: (801) 378-6347.

Gail King, Curator

Year started: 1972

Hours:

Monday-Saturday: 7:00 am - Midnight
Holidays and intersessions: 8:00 am - 6:00 pm

Holdings:

Total CJK volumes:	61,266
Current serials:	
Chinese:	78
Japanese:	16
Korean:	8
Current newspapers:	
Chinese:	2
Japanese:	1
Korean:	1

Areas of strength:

Chinese, Japanese, and Korean materials in the humanities and social sciences are collected to support the university curriculum and faculty research in East Asian studies.

Special collections:

The library's Special Collections Department has some Edo and Meiji period Japanese materials which include 200 books and maps, 25 scrolls, and 20 wood-block prints.

Access:

Library is open to the public. The library participates in the OCLC Reciprocal Faculty Borrowing Program for resource sharing among research libraries.

Interlibrary loan service:

Available to all libraries.

Online cataloging:

East Asian materials are cataloged in the RLIN CJK system.

Catalogs for use of the Collection:

Card Catalogs: East Asian card catalogs are maintained but closed since 1983. However, the shelflist card catalog is still being maintained.

Online Catalog: The local online catalog, BYLINE, started to include romanized East Asian records in 1982.

Network/Consortium affiliation:

Member of RLG.

4. UNIVERSITY OF BRITISH COLUMBIA

Asian Studies Library, Asian Centre, 1871 West Mall
Vancouver, B.C., Canada V6T 1W5
Tel: (604) 228-2427. FAX: (604) 228-5207.

Linda Joe, Head

Year founded: 1960

Hours:

Monday-Thursday: 8:30 am - 8:00 pm	Summer:
Friday: 8:30 am - 5:00 pm	Monday-Friday:
Saturday: Noon - 5:00 pm	9:00 am - 5:00 pm

Holdings:

Volumes:
Chinese:	195,308
Japanese:	100,041
Korean:	6,515

Current serials:
Chinese:	886
Japanese:	1,373
Korean:	63

Current newspapers:
Chinese:	19
Japanese:	7
Korean:	2

East Asian microfilm reels and fiche cards: 21,505

Areas of strength:

The library has the largest collection of East Asian materials in Canada, with most of the holdings in Chinese and Japanese. The collection covers a full range of subjects in the humanities and social sciences, and is particularly strong in history, literature, Japanese statistics and economy, and religious studies, particularly Buddhist studies. In addition to East Asian materials, the library has also a rich collection of books from South Asia and Indonesia.

Special collections:

1. P'u-pan Collection: 45,000 volumes of Chinese printed books and unpublished manuscripts dated before 1912, of which 115 are from the Sung and Yuan dynasties (960-1368), 3,326 from Ming (1368-1644) and 9,865 from Ch'ing (1644-1911) dynasties. Some of the notable items include a 986 edition of the *Shuo wen wu yin yun pu*; local gazetteers of the Kwangtung Province, and literary writings by Kwangtung authors.

2. Japanese government publications: As the only full depository of Japanese government publications in Canada, the Asian Library holds a rich collection (over 26,000 items) of Japanese official gazettes, white papers, statistical reports, statutes, publications on Japanese science and technology, etc.

3. George H. Beans Collection of Japanese Maps: 320 sets of rare maps of Japan produced between 1600 and 1867, many of which are woodblock prints and in color. The collection contains works of prominent Ukiyo-e artists such as Moronobu, Hokusai, Hiroshige, and Sadahide.

4. Asian-Canadian Archives: Over 90 collections of archival materials pertaining to the history of Chinese and Japanese immigrants in Canada, evacuation of the Japanese-Canadians from the West Coast and their ensuing experience, history of Chinese workers in various industries, and other related topics. There are more than 41 feet of unpublished documents and over 1,400 pieces of photographs, clippings, journals, cassette tapes, and other non-book items.

East Asian materials in other collections:

The Beans Collection and the Asian-Canadian Archives described above are housed in the Special Collections Division in the Main Library. Japanese legal periodicals are in the Law Library.

Access:

The library is open to the public. Borrowing privileges are given to the following:

a) UBC faculty, students, staff, and members of the community
b) Off-campus users who hold extra-mural cards (may borrow books, but not serials)

     c)   Visiting faculty who hold an OCLC Reciprocal Faculty Borrowing Card

     d)   Graduate students in Southeast Asian studies from the University of Washington and the University of Oregon (under the term of the Northwest Regional Consortium for Southeast Asian Studies, of which UBC is a member)

Interlibrary loan service:

Books are lent to Canadian and U.S. libraries only.

Online cataloging:

The library started to catalog its East Asian materials in the RLIN CJK system in February 1991. Its brief romanized records have been loaded in UTLAS since 1978 and in OCLC since 1987.

Catalogs for use of the collection:

Card Catalogs: East Asian card catalogs are maintained.

Online Catalog: The local online catalog, UBCLIB, includes brief romanized records for CJK materials cataloged as of January, 1978.

Network/Consortium affiliation:

Member of RLG and the Northwest Regional Consortium for Southeast Asian Studies.

Publications:

    1. *Periodicals in Asian Studies in the University of British Columbia Library*, prepared by the Asian Studies Library. 3rd ed. Vancouver, B.C.: University of British Columbia, 1978.

    2. *Union List of Current Japanese Serials in Six East Asian Libraries of Western North America* (British Columbia, U.C.-Berkeley, UCLA, Hawaii, Hoover, and Washington), compiled by Mihoko Miki. [Los Angeles]: Western Regional Japanese Library Conference, 1988.

5. BROWN UNIVERSITY

> East Asian Collection, Rockefeller Library
> Providence, Rhode Island 02912
> Tel: (401) 863-2171

Year started: 1961

Hours:

> Monday-Thursday: 8:30 am - 2:00 am
> Friday: 8:30 am - 10:00 pm
> Saturday: 9:00 am - 10:00 pm
> Sunday: Noon - 2:00 am

Holdings:

> Volumes:
>
> | | |
> |---|---|
> | Chinese: | 93,000 |
> | Japanese: | 4,800 |
> | Korean: | 1,500 |

Areas of strength:

The collection focuses on materials for Chinese studies. Current emphases in acquisitions are on language, literature, history, religion and philosophy, fine arts, and politics and government.

Special collections:

The Charles Sidney Gardner Collection contains 20,000 volumes on Chinese history and philosophy, most of which relate to the Ch'ing dynasty (1644-1912).

Access:

The library is open to the public. However, individuals entering the library need to show Brown University IDs, a current access or borrowing card, or other specific card or referral letter. Standard annual fees are $50 for the access card and $300 for the borrowing card. There are special rules and regulations governing borrowing privileges for visiting scholars and faculty and students from other institutions. (Inquiries regarding use of the library should be directed to the library's Circulation Department.)

Interlibrary loan service:

Available to all libraries.

Online cataloging:

East Asian materials are cataloged in the RLIN CJK system.

Catalogs for use of the collection:

Card Catalogs: East Asian card catalogs are maintained.

Network/Consortium affiliation:

Member of RLG.

6. UNIVERSITY OF CALIFORNIA, BERKELEY

East Asian Library, 208 Durant Hall, Berkeley, California 94720
Tel: (510) 642-2556. FAX: (510) 643-7891.

Donald H. Shively, Head

Year founded: 1947

Hours:

Monday-Thursday: 9:00 am - 7:00 pm	Summer & intercessions:
Friday: 9:00 am - 5:00 pm	Monday - Friday:
Saturday-Sunday: 1:00 - 5:00 pm	9:00 am - 5:00 pm

Holdings:

Volumes:
Chinese:	292,593
Japanese:	280,379
Korean:	37,944

Current serials:
Chinese:	1,894
Japanese:	1,857
Korean:	426

Current newspapers:
Chinese:	80
Japanese:	14
Korean:	7

East Asian microfilm reels and fiche cards: 12,086

Areas of strength:

The library has a very comprehensive collection of books and other library materials in East Asian languages, with great strength in the humanities and social sciences.   Strong subject areas are: language, literature, archaeology, history, philosophy, fine arts, religion, politics, economic and social conditions, ethnology, and cultural traits and customs.

The Center for Chinese Studies Library, located at 2223 Fulton Street, is a branch of the East Asian Library. It collects materials on contemporary Chinese government, politics, economic and social conditions, and post-1949 Chinese Communist Party. Its holdings include 45,457 volumes (mostly in Chinese); 1,400 periodicals and newspapers; 3,900 reels of microfilm (including the Union Research Institute newspaper clipping file); more than 200 yearbooks; 1,460 volumes of the *Wen shih tzu liao* series, several hundred volumes of which are not available elsewhere outside China; and some periodicals published by Red Guards during the Cultural Revolution. The center library's other special materials include the JPRS (Joint Publication Research Service) translations, transcripts of FBIS (Foreign Broadcast Information Service) and BBC foreign radio, and more than 400 video tapes of news programs and documentaries broadcast from Beijing.

In addition to CJK materials, the East Asian Library has also extensive holdings in Tibetan, Mongolian, and Manchu.

Special collections:

1. The Asami Library of Korean rare books in wood-block print, movable-type, and manuscript editions, 900 titles in 4,310 volumes, and also Korean rubbings.

2. Chinese rubbings, 2,741 sheets from the Mitsui and other collections.

3. Edo period wood-block printed books, 5,013 titles (over 18,000 volumes) from the Gakken, Motoori, Soshin, and Kihon collections of the Mitsui Library.

4. The Murakami Library of over 10,000 volumes of literary works by Meiji authors, almost all in first editions. There are also several thousand Meiji editions from the Mitsui Library.

5. Early Japanese maps, including 726 Edo period maps, mostly wood-block printed, and 1,667 Meiji maps, which have been cataloged in RLIN. There are also three pairs of Edo period map screens.

6. Japanese manuscripts of literary and historical texts from the Mitsui Library, 2,877 titles in 7,000 volumes.

7. The Chinese rare book collection includes 17 Sung, 25 yuan, 357 Ming, and 529 Ch'ing titles.

8. The Ho-Chiang Collection of 110 Chinese, Japanese and Korean manuscripts and printed editions of Buddhist scriptures, dating from the eighth to the eighteenth century.

9. The Mongolian and Manchu collections with an exceedingly rare Manchu title, *Tai sang-ni acabume karulara bithe*, published in 1673.

10. The Tibetan collection which consists of xylographs printed in Tibet before 1949, including a corpus of Tantric texts of the Nying-ma-pa Sect spanning ten centuries of composition and a set of the 18th century Narthang edition of the Kanjur section of the Buddhist canon.

11. Japanese titles from the 19th century in 522 volumes.

East Asian materials in other collections:

There is a significant number of books in East Asian languages in the Environmental Design Library, and a collection of Chinese and Japanese children's picture books in the Education/Psychology Library. The Lowie Museum of Anthropology has four Oracle bones. The Map Room has 14,000 modern maps of Japan and East Asia.

Access:

The library is open to the public. Borrowing privileges are given to all University of California system faculty and students with IDs or library cards. Other faculty and researchers may apply for courtesy cards.

Interlibrary loan service:

Available to all libraries.

Online cataloging:

East Asian materials have been cataloged in the RLIN CJK system since July 1989.

Catalogs for use of the collection:

Card Catalogs: East Asian card catalogs are maintained but closed since 1989. Currently only title and shelflist cards are filed.

Online Catalog: The local online catalogs, GLADIS and MELVYL, contain East Asian records in romanization only.

Network/Consortium affiliation:

Member of RLG and the Western Regional Japanese Library Conference.

Publications:

1. *Author-Title Catalog*, East Asiatic Library, University of California, Berkeley. Boston: G. K. Hall, 1968. 13 v. *Supplement*, 1973. 2 v.

2. *Subject Catalog*, East Asiatic Library, University of California, Berkeley. Boston: G. K. Hall, 1968. 6 v. *First Supplement*, 1973. 2 v.

3. *The Asami Library: A Descriptive Catalogue*, by Chaoying Fang. Berkeley and Los Angeles: University of California Press, 1969.

4. *The Korean Buddhist Canon: A Descriptive Catalog*, by Lewis R. Lancaster, in collaboration with Sung-bae Park. Berkeley and Los Angeles: University of California Press, 1979.

5. "Karifuorunia Daigaku Bakure-ko Kyu-Mitsui Bunko shahon mokuroku ko" (Catalog of manuscripts of the former Mitsui Library at the University of California, Berkeley).   Kokubungaku Kenkyu Shiryokan Bunken Shiryo-bu, *Chosa Kenkyu Hokoku* No. 5 (March 1984): 261-340.

6. *A Checklist of Japanese Government Publications: East Asiatic Library, University of California, Berkeley, and East Asian Collection, Hoover Institution, Stanford University* (Kashu Daigaku Bakure-ko oyobi Sutanfuodo Daigaku Shozo Nihon seifu kankobutsu mokuroku), edited by Akifumi Oikawa, Eiji Yutani, and Emiko Mashiko Moffitt. Tokyo: Kinokuniya Shoten, 1987. 2 v.

7. *Edo Printed Books at Berkeley (Kashu Daigaku Bakure-ko shozo Mitsui Bunko kyuzo) Edo hanpon shomoku*, edited by Oka Masahiko, Kodama Fumiko, Tozawa Ikuko, and Ishimatsu Hisayuki. Tokyo: Yumani Shobo, 1990.

8. *Union List of Current Japanese Serials in Six East Asian Libraries of Western North America* (British Columbia, U.C.-Berkeley, UCLA, Hawaii,

Hoover, and Washington), compiled by Mihoko Miki. [Los Angeles]: Western Regional Japanese Library Conference, 1988.

9. *Checking List of the Periodicals by Red Guards*, Center for Chinese Studies Library. 1968.

10. Checklists of the holdings of the Berkeley and Stanford collections, published jointly:

> *A Checklist of Japanese Company Histories* (1978)
> *A Checklist of Japanese Local Histories* (1978)
> *A Checklist of Japanese Newspapers* (1978)
> *Union List of Chinese Periodicals* (1978)
> *A Checklist of Chinese Local Histories* (1980)
> *A Checklist of Chinese Newspapers* (1986)

7. UNIVERSITY OF CALIFORNIA, DAVIS

Asian Languages Collection, Shields Library
Davis, California 95616-5292
Tel: (916) 752-0594. FAX: (916) 752-6899.

Phyllis Wang
Collection Development Librarian and Acquisitions Assistant

Year started: 1967

Hours:

Weekdays: 8:00 am - Midnight
Weekends: 10:00 am - 11:00 pm

Holdings:

Volumes:

Chinese:	29,129
Japanese:	14,345
Korean:	379

Current serials:

Chinese:	83
Japanese:	47
Korean:	3

Current newspapers:

Chinese:	7
Japanese:	4
Korean:	2

Chinese and Japanese microfilm reels and fiche cards: 179

Areas of strength:

The collection contains mainly Chinese and Japanese vernacular materials in humanities and social sciences. Collection strengths are in these subject areas: History, language, literature, fine arts, and reference works. For Chinese studies, the collection is strong in the history of the Ch'ing period, modern Chinese literature, and Chinese art history.

East Asian materials in other collections:

The Chinese and Japanese Programs on campus maintain a small collection of teaching materials and films.

Access:

The library is open to the public. Faculty, students, staff, and members who have paid for the borrowing privileges can check out materials.

Interlibrary loan service:

Available to all libraries.

Online cataloging:

East Asian materials are cataloged in the general RLIN database, with records in romanization only.

Catalogs for use of the Collection:

Card Catalogs: East Asian card catalogs are maintained.

Online Catalog: Since May 1985, East Asian romanized records have been included in the local online catalog, MELVYL.

Network/Consortium affiliation:

Member of RLG.

8. UNIVERSITY OF CALIFORNIA, IRVINE

East Asian Collection, University Library, P.O. Box 19557
Irvine, California 92713
Tel: (714) 856-8147. FAX: (714) 856-5740.

William Sheh Wong, East Asian Librarian

Year started: 1990

Hours:

Monday-Thursday: 8:00 am - Midnight
Friday: 8:00 am - 6:00 pm
Saturday: Noon - 6:00 pm
Sundays: Noon - Midnight

Holdings:

Volumes:
Chinese:	16,000
Japanese:	1,500
Chinese and Japanese serials:	50

Areas of strength:

This is a newly started collection with a focus on Chinese and Japanese literature and history.

Access:

The library is open to the public. Holders of a U.C.-Irvine library card may check out books. There are two kinds of library cards: courtesy cards (for U.C. system faculty and students) and fee cards which range from $24 (for non-U.C. system students) to $50 (for all others) per year.

Interlibrary loan service:

Available to all libraries.

Online cataloging:

East Asian materials are cataloged in the OCLC CJK system.

Catalogs for use of the Collection:

Card Catalogs: East Asian card catalogs are maintained.

Network/Consortium affiliation:

Member of OCLC.

9. UNIVERSITY OF CALIFORNIA, LOS ANGELES

Richard C. Rudolph East Asian Library, 405 Hilgard Avenue
Los Angeles, California 90024
Tel: (213) 825-1401. FAX: (213) 206-3374.

James K. M. Cheng, Head

Year founded: 1948

Hours:

Monday-Thursday: 8:00 am - 9:00 pm
Friday-Saturday: 9:00 am - 5:00 pm
Sunday: 1:00 pm - 5:00 pm

Holdings:

Volumes:

Chinese:	162,496
Japanese:	115,251
Korean:	15,424

Serials and newspapers:

Chinese:	1,287
Japanese:	873
Korean:	214

East Asian microfilm reels and fiche cards: 5,475

Areas of strength:

The library has strong and extensive holdings in East Asian humanities and social sciences. Its subject strengths lie in Chinese and Japanese fine arts, Chinese archaeology, religion, Buddhism, ancient history and classical literature of China and Japan, and Korean literature and religion. The library's holdings on Japanese Buddhism are very comprehensive.

Special collections:

1. Han Yu-shan Collection of Chinese imperial examination papers.

2. Collection of K'ang Yu-wei on overseas Chinese and the 1911 Revolution.

3. Rare Japanese maps of the Edo period.

4. Collection of rare materials on both Chinese and Japanese medical history.

5. The Julian Wright Collection of rare titles on Japanese art, especially those of the Edo period.

East Asian materials in other collections:

Collection on Chinese and Japanese medical history at the Biomedical Library. Strong collection of source materials on Japanese Americans at the Department of Special Collections. The Law Library has 5,330 volumes of East Asian legal materials and about 170 current serials and newspapers.

Access:

The library is open to the public. Through cooperative arrangements, the UCLA Library is open, with borrowing privileges, to the faculty and students of other University of California campuses in southern California (e.g. Santa Barbara, Irvine, San Diego, and Riverside) and those of the University of Southern California and the California Institute of Technology.

Interlibrary loan service:

Available to all libraries.

Online cataloging:

East Asian materials are cataloged in the OCLC CJK system.

Catalogs for use of the Collection:

Card Catalogs: East Asian card catalogs are maintained.

Online Catalog: East Asian records, in romanized form, are included in the local online catalog, MELVYL. In addition, all East Asian serial titles are now in UCLA's online system: ORION.

Network/Consortium affiliation:

Member of OCLC, Southern California Library Consortium for Japanese Studies (with U.C.-San Diego), and UCLA and USC Joint Center in East Asian Studies.

Publications:

1. *Dictionary Catalog of the University Library, 1919-1962*, Library of the University of California, Los Angeles. Boston: G.K. Hall, 1063. Vols. 127-128: Chinese Collection; vol. 129: Japanese Collection.

2. *Union List of Current Japanese Serials in Six East Asian Libraries of Western North America* (British Columbia, U.C.-Berkeley, UCLA, Hawaii, Hoover, and Washington), compiled by Mihoko Miki. [Los Angeles]: Western Regional Japanese Library Conference, 1988.

10. UNIVERSITY OF CALIFORNIA, SAN DIEGO

International Relations and Pacific Studies Library
La Jolla, California 92093-0175
Tel: (619) 534-7788. FAX: (619) 534-4970.

Karl K. Lo, Head

Year founded: 1987

Hours:

Weekdays: 8:00 am - 10:00 pm
Friday: 8:00 am - 6:00 pm
Saturday: 9:00 am - 5:00 pm
Sunday: 1:00 pm - 10:00 pm

Holdings: (as of October 31, 1990)

Volumes:
Chinese:	17,306
Japanese:	10,622
Korean:	125
Current serials:
Chinese:	271
Japanese:	295
Korean:	12
Current newspapers:
Chinese:	12
Japanese:	5
Korean:	3
East Asian microfilm reels and fiche cards:	106

Areas of strength:

The International Relations and Pacific Studies Library is a newly established library with a strong collection emphasis on social sciences including economics, business, and international relations with East Asian countries. The general library of the university has a long history of collecting CJK materials in the humanities including history, language and literature, philosophy, religion, etc.

Access:

The library is open to the public. Borrowing privileges are given to faculty and students of the University of California campuses and the State university system. Others may obtain borrowing privileges by paying a fee or through special arrangements.

Interlibrary loan service:

Available to all libraries.

Online cataloging:

East Asian materials are cataloged in the OCLC CJK system.

Catalogs for use of the Collection:

Card Catalogs: East Asian card catalogs are maintained.

Online Catalog: The local online catalog, ROGER, includes all East Asian materials in romanized form.

11. UNIVERSITY OF CALIFORNIA, SANTA BARBARA

East Asian Studies Collection, University Library
Santa Barbara, California 93106
Tel: (805) 893-2365. FAX: (805) 893-4676.

Cathy Chiu, East Asian Librarian

Year started: 1967

Hours:

Monday-Friday: 8:00 am - 5:00 pm
Weekends: Closed

Holdings:

Volumes:
Chinese:	53,985
Japanese:	33,188
Korean:	104

Current serials:
Chinese:	276
Japanese:	222
Korean:	4

Current newspapers:
Chinese:	9
Japanese:	5
Korean:	4

Chinese and Japanese microfilm reels and fiche cards: 1,653

Areas of strength:

East Asian materials in the humanities and social sciences are collected. Strong subject areas of the collection are: History, political science, art, religious studies, and Chinese and Japanese language and literature.

Access:

Library is open to the public. Borrowing privileges are given to all faculty, staff and students who are entitled to a library card. The library card can be issued to anyone outside the university with a fee.

Interlibrary loan service:

Available to all libraries.

Online Cataloging:

East Asian materials are cataloged in the RLIN. CJK system.

Catalogs for use of the Collection:

Card Catalogs: East Asian card catalogs are maintained.

Online Catalog: East Asian records are included in the local online catalog, MELVYL, in romanized form.

Network/Consortium affiliation:

Member of RLIN.

12. CENTER FOR RESEARCH LIBRARIES

6050 South Kenwood Avenue, Chicago, Illinois 60673
Tel: (312) 955-4545. (800) 621-6044.
FAX: (312) 955-4339

Ray Boylan, Director, Collection Resources

Year founded: 1949

Hours:

Weekdays: 9:00 am - 5:00 pm
Weekends: Closed

Holdings:

Estimated East Asian volumes: 12,400. Estimated East Asian microfilm reels: 14,000.

Areas of strength:

East Asian materials held at the Center consists primarily of microform and reprint sets that are rarely held in North America. Particularly strong are the microform collections of archival materials, government documents, and newspapers. The Center has also a very strong collection of U.S. State Department and British Foreign Office records relating to China, Japan and Korea, as well as a strong collection of China coast newspapers in Western languages.   In addition, it maintains approximately 600 subscriptions to Japanese science and technology journals.

Special collections:

Major special collections at the Center include the following:

1.   The Hunter Collection contains Chinese Communist publications, newspaper clippings, news releases, etc. collected by Edward Hunter as source materials for his books: *Brain Washing in Red China* and *The Story of Mary Liu*.

2. Chinese Folk Literature on Microfilm: 232 reels of Chinese folk literature collected and cataloged by the Academia Sinica, Taiwan.

3. Survived Books of Tun-huang: A 144-reel microfilm set, made by the National Library of China, Beijing, consists of manuscripts, mostly from the period of the T'ang dynasty, that were found in the Tun-huang grottoes.

4. Union Research Institute files of about 2,000 microfilm reels of newspapers, periodicals, and classified files published in China between 1949 and 1966.

5. Japanese Cabinet archives, the Dajo ruiten (1876-1881) and Kobun ruiju (1882-1885) on 250 microfilm reels; and the Japanese Ministry of Foreign Affairs archives (1868-1945) on 2,117 reels made by the Library of Congress, 1949-1951.

Access:

Faculty, students, and other researchers may visit the Center's reading room to use Center materials. Arrangements must be made with the Circulation Department in advance of the patron's visit to insure that needed materials are available. On site borrowing is not allowed. All borrowing must be through interlibrary loans.

Interlibrary loan service:

Available to the Center's about 150 member institutions in North America. Non-member libraries have limited borrowing privileges for a prepaid transaction fee.

Online Cataloging:

East Asian materials are cataloged in the OCLC system. Records are in romanized form only. The Center's catalog tapes are also loaded in RLIN.

Catalogs for use of the Collection:

Card Catalogs: East Asian catalog cards are maintained but interfiled in the Center's general catalog.

Publications:

1. *The Center for Research Libraries Handbook.* 1990.

2. *East Asian Materials: A Brief Introduction for Researchers at Member Libraries.*

3. *East Asian Serials Currently Received at the Center for Research Libraries.* 1984.

13. UNIVERSITY OF CHICAGO

East Asian Library, Joseph Regenstein Library
Chicago, Illinois 60637-1502
Tel: (312) 702-8432. FAX: (312) 702-0853.

Tai-loi Ma, Curator

Year founded: 1936

Hours:

Monday-Thursday: 9:00 am - 10:00 pm
Friday-Saturday: 9:00 am - 5:00 pm
Summer: 9:00 am - 5:00 pm (weekdays)
Intersessions: 9:00 am - 1:00 pm (weekdays)

Holdings:

Volumes:
    Chinese: 296,473
    Japanese: 140,394
    Korean: 9,115
Current serials:
    Chinese: 1,310
    Japanese: 1,896
    Korean: 387
Current newspapers:
    Chinese: 59
    Japanese: 16
    Korean: 5
East Asian microfilm reels and fiche cards: 22,528

Areas of strength:

The library's Chinese collection is specially strong in classics, philosophy, history, local histories, archaeology, art, and literature. The Japanese collection has distinguished holdings in literature, history, fine arts, history of religions, and sinology. The Korean collection is relatively young and small, but is growing rapidly.

Special collections:

1. A large Chinese rare books collection (over 1,400 titles).

2. The Laufer Collection contains about 7,000 volumes in Manchu, Mongolian, and Tibetan.

Access:

The library is open to the public. A day pass, a reference privilege card or a borrowing privilege card is needed for admission to the library. Borrowing privileges are given to faculty and students of the university, and to faculty of the eleven Midwest CIC member universities. Others may use the library by paying a fee or by special permissions. Special extended use of the collection is permitted for students from members of the RLG East Asian studies program.

Travel grants:

Travel grants for out-of-state users of the collection, up to $250 per user, is available. Special consideration will be given to those residing in the Midwest and in areas where no major East Asian collections are available.

Interlibrary loan service:

Available to all libraries.

Online cataloging:

East Asian materials are cataloged in the RLIN CJK system.

Catalogs for use of the collection:

Card Catalogs: East Asian card catalogs are maintained.

Network/Consortium affiliation:

Member of RLG, Midwest Library Consortium (with the University of Michigan), and CIC.

Publications:

1. *Catalogues of the Far Eastern Library.* Chicago: University of Chicago, 1973. 18 v. *Supplements*, 1981. 12 v.

2. *Far Eastern Serials.* Chicago: Far Eastern Library, University of Chicago Library, 1977.

3. *Chinese Local Histories.* Chicago: Far Eastern Library, University of Chicago Library, 1969.

14. CLAREMONT COLLEGES

Asian Studies Collection, Honnold Library
Claremont, California 91711
Tel: (714) 621-8000 Ext. 3970

Year started: 1933

Hours:

Monday-Friday: 8:15 am - Noon; 1:00 pm - 4:45 pm
Weekends: Closed

Holdings:

Volumes:
Chinese:		58,160
Japanese:		11,198
Korean:		957

Current serials:
Chinese:		189
Japanese:		38
Korean:		7

Current newspapers:
Chinese:		5
Japanese:		2

Chinese microfilm reels and fiche cards: 104

Areas of strength:

East Asian materials in the humanities and social sciences are collected. The Chinese collection contains materials on history, language and literature, archaeology, basic reference books, and special materials the most distinguished of which is the collection of some two hundred titles of Chinese local gazetteers. The Japanese collection consists of basic reference books, major literary works, histories, and, especially, biographical materials.

Rare items owned by the collection include a book on medical science, *Su wen ju shih yun ch'i lun ao*, in two volumes with a preface dated 1909 and reprinted in the Ming dynasty; and a manuscript set of the four classics, *Ssu shu t'u shuo*, in nineteen stitched volumes bound in yellow silk covers and protected by four yellow silk covered cases. The latter is a handwritten manuscript, written by imperial order of the Ch'ing emperor

Kuang-hsu toward the end of his reign (1904-06) and is one of only two copies ever produced.

Special collection:

The California College in China Collection consists of about five hundred titles of works in history, literature, and local gazetteers, all original Ming, Ch'ing, or early. 19th century editions.

East Asian materials in other collections:

The Frederick McCormick Korean Collection in the Special Collections Department contains hundreds of volumes of rare Korean books, printed with movable-type, of Chinese classics, historical studies, humanities and sciences, literary anthologies, and rubbings of tomb memorials.

Access:

The library is open to the public. Borrowing privileges are given to local faculty, students, and staff and also to outside users.

Interlibrary loan service:

Available to all libraries.

Online Cataloging:

The library is still doing manual cataloging.

Catalogs for use of the Collection:

Card Catalogs: East Asian card catalogs are maintained.

15. UNIVERSITY OF COLORADO, BOULDER

East Asiatic Library, Campus Box 184
Boulder, Colorado 80309-0184
Tel: (303) 492-8822. FAX: (303) 492-2185.

Year started: 1989

Hours:

Weekdays: 8:00 am - Midnight   Friday: 8:00 am - 5:00 pm
Saturday: 10:00 am - Midnight   Saturday: 10:00 am - 5:00 pm
Sunday: Noon - Midnight   Sunday: Noon - 10 pm
Summer:
Monday-Thursday: 8:00 am - 10:00 pm

Holdings:

Volumes:
    Chinese: 17,305
    Japanese: 3,328
    Korean: 11
Current CJK serials and newspapers: 63

Areas of strength:

The collection is predominately Chinese. It focuses on Chinese sinology, history, and literature (particularly literature of the T'ang and Sung periods). Special collections include about forty rare titles of Chinese classic literature and some major Chinese collections such as the *Ssu k'u ch'uan shu, Pai pu ts'ung shu chi ch'eng, Ssu pu pei yao*, etc.

Access:

The library is open to the public. Patrons can check out materials with a library card which is available to all with a current valid ID.

Interlibrary loan service:

Available to all libraries.

Online cataloging:

East Asian materials are cataloged in the OCLC CJK system.

Catalogs for use of the collection:

Card catalogs: East Asian card catalogs are maintained.

Online catalog: The local online catalog, CARL, contains East Asian records in romanized form only.

Network/Consortium affiliation:

Member of OCLC and CARL.

16. COLUMBIA UNIVERSITY

C. V. Starr East Asian Library, 300 Kent Hall
New York, New York 10027
Tel: (212) 854-2578. FAX: (212) 662-6286.

Amy Vladeck Heinrich, Acting East Asian Librarian

Year founded: 1902

Hours:

Monday-Thursday: 9:00 am - 11:00 pm
Friday: 9:00 am - 7:00 pm
Saturday: Noon - 7:00 pm
Sunday: Noon - 10:00 pm

Special Collections Reading Room hours:
Mondays and Wednesdays: 2:00 pm - 4:00 pm
Tuesdays and Thursdays: 10:00 am - 12:00 pm

Holdings:

Volumes:	
Chinese:	262,066
Japanese:	203,253
Korean:	35,462
Current serials:	
Chinese:	1,745
Japanese:	1,002
Korean:	280
Current newspapers:	
Chinese:	24
Japanese:	10
Korean:	7
Western:	6
East Asian microfilm reels and fiche cards:	26,428

Areas of strength:

The East Asian collection contains over 500,000 volumes in the Chinese, Japanese, Korean, Manchu and Mongolian languages, as well as a large collection of Western-language secondary materials and translations.

The Chinese collection, which is the largest, is strongest in history, literature, and thought. It includes one of the largest collections of original editions of gazetteers and genealogies outside China. The Collection is also strong in Ming and Ch'ing belles lettres. The Japanese collection is strong in traditional history, literature, Buddhism, philosophy, and is growing rapidly in the social sciences. The Korean collection is strong in traditional history, literature, philosophy, and religion.

Special collections:

The Rare Books and Special Collections include these major holdings:

Chinese:

A core collection of about 800 titles in 5,000 volumes dating from before the 60th year of the Ch'ien-lung reign (1795); many of the finest items are Ming dynasty works. These include 22 titles of Ming books banned by the Ch'ing government and therefore very rare; some are unique. The strongest areas of the collection are family genealogies and local gazetteers. Other materials in the collection include 67 Oracle bones, from 1400-1100 B.C.; 85 Manchu titles in 644 volumes published in the Ch'ing dynasty; and some Tibetan language research materials and Mongolian translations of Chinese literature.

Archives: Archival materials on the Chinese Democracy Movement of 1989, which include more than 600 original and copies of leaflets and handbills, 200 plus photographs of big character posters and student demonstrations, over 20 eyewitness accounts of the June 4 crackdown, etc. A collection of Red Guards publications from the Chinese Cultural Revolution. The Morton H. Fried Collection of anthropological field notes, correspondence; and working reports.

Japanese:

The core of the collection includes Edo and Meiji period wood-block printed books, particularly those from the 14th through 19th centuries, and gift books from the Imperial Household Ministry in the late 1920s. The collection also contains some special holdings including early movable-type editions; many *utaibon*; and Tokugawa editions of Japanese literature. The Donald Keene Collection of Twentieth Century Japanese Literature has many first editions inscribed by the authors to Donald Keene.

Korean:

The Korean rare book collection includes the Yi Song-ui Collection of 517 titles in 1,857 volumes, on paekchi paper. Of these, approximately 100 volumes are very early examples of moveable-type printed books from the 16th century, and over 900 volumes are classic Yi dynasty language and literature books. The collection also includes Yi dynasty official gazettes, the Pannam Pak family genealogies, and modern Korean fiction.

East Asian materials in other collections:

The Law Library holds materials in Chinese and Japanese. The Chinese Oral History Project of the East Asian Institute has a collection of oral histories of prominent Chinese of the modern period.

Access:

The C. V. Starr Library is open to users for in-house use of books. The portion of the collection separately housed in the Annex is available by arrangement with the Head of Reference and Resource Services. Borrowing privileges are available for fees established by the University, and may be arranged with the Library Information Office, 234 Butler Library.

Non-circulating materials in the Rare Book and Special Collections are available for use only in the Special Collections Reading Room which is open Monday and Wednesday, 2:00 - 4:00 pm and Tuesday and Thursday, 10:00 am - 12:00 pm.

Interlibrary loan service:

Available to all libraries.

Online cataloging:

East Asian materials are cataloged in the RLIN CJK system.

Catalogs for use of the Collection:

Card Catalogs: East Asian card catalogs are maintained.

Online Catalog: The local online catalog, CLIO (Columbia Libraries Information Online), contains all Columbia records for everything cataloged from 1982 on, as well as many pre-1982 materials. CJK records in CLIO are in romanized form only. Approximately 12% of the East Asian collection is on line.

Network/Consortium affiliation:

Member of the East Coast East Asian Library Consortium (Japanese: Columbia, Harvard, Princeton and Yale. Chinese: Columbia, Cornell, Harvard, New York Public Library, Princeton and Yale), RLG, and METRO (a cooperative consortium of New York Metropolitan Area Libraries).

Publications:

1. *C.V. Starr East Asian Library: Columbia University, April 27, 1983.* New York: Columbia University, 1983.

2. *Union List of Japanese Periodicals in the East Asian Libraries of Columbia, Harvard, Princeton, and Yale Universities*, second edition, 1989; bilingual.

3. *The Chinese Oral History Project.* New York: The East Asian Institute of Columbia University, 1972.

17. CORNELL UNIVERSITY

Wason Collection, Onlin Library
Ithaca, New York 14853-5301
Tel: (607) 255-4357. FAX: (607) 255-9091.

Year started: 1919

Hours:

Monday-Thursday: 8:00 am - Midnight
Friday: 8:00 am - 6:00 pm
Saturday: 9:00 am - 6:00 pm
Sunday: 1:00 pm - Midnight

Holdings:

Volumes:
Chinese: 257,571
Japanese: 63,965
Current serial:
Chinese: 1,449
Japanese: 405
Korean: 18
Current newspapers:
Chinese: 15
Japanese: 3
Korean: 1
East Asian microfilm reels and fiche cards: 12,205

Areas of strength:

The Wason Collection contains extensive materials on China and Japan, and some materials on Korea, and has greater strength in the subject areas of fine arts, humanities, and social sciences (particularly law, business, and economics). The collection is known for its rich holdings of post-1949 materials on mainland China, twentieth century Chinese publications, and Ming and Ch'ing fiction.

Special collections:

1. Tun-huang manuscripts of Pelliot and Stein (microfilm).

2. The Rev. William E. Griffis Collection of 18th and 19th century materials on Japan.

3. Collection of manuscripts and original papers of Lord Macartney about his mission to China in 1793.

4. A collection of about 179 titles of folk literature including the *mu-yu-shu*.

Access:

The Olin Library has a closed stacks policy. The Circulation Department will get books for patrons who request them. Users can also request a stack pass at Circulation so that they may get the books themselves. Patrons affiliated with Cornell (i.e. staff, faculty, and students) may check out materials. Others who wish to borrow materials from the library may obtain a library card, with a fee, from the Circulation Department.

Interlibrary loan service:

Available to most libraries.

Online cataloging:

East Asian materials are cataloged in the RLIN CJK system

Catalogs for use of the Collection:

Card Catalogs: East Asian card catalogs are maintained.

Network/Consortium affiliation:

Member of RLG and the East Coast East Asian Consortium (for Chinese).

Publications:

1. *Catalog of the Wason Collection on China and the Chinese.* Washington, D.C.: Center for Chinese Research Materials, Association of Research Libraries, 1980. 9 v.

2.   *The Griffis Collection of Japanese Books: An Annotated Bibliography*, edited by D. E. Perushek. Ithaca, N.Y.: China-Japan Program, Cornell University, 1982.

3.   Howard, Richard C.   "Wason Collection on China and the Chinese," *Cornell University Library Bulletin* 193 (January 1975): 36-43.

18. DARTMOUTH COLLEGE

Oriental Collection, Baker Library
Hanover, New Hampshire 03755
Tel: (603) 646-2568. FAX: (603) 646-3702.

John R. James
Director of Collection Development and Bibliographic Control

Year stated: 1967

Hours:

Weekdays: 8:00 am - Midnight
Weekends: 8:00 am - 6:00 pm

Holdings:

Total volumes in Chinese and Japanese: 25,000. Current serials and newspapers: 90.

Areas of strength:

The Collection is predominately Chinese. Japanese titles are being added since 1990. The holdings are strongest in history and literature.

Access:

The library is open to the public. Borrowing privileges are given to any member of the Dartmouth Community and any graduate student or faculty from an RLG institution (with current ID). Others may purchase library cards for using the library.

Interlibrary loan service:

Available to all libraries.

Online cataloging:

East Asian materials are cataloged in the RLIN CJK system

Catalogs for use of the Collection:

Card Catalogs: East Asian card catalogs are maintained

Online Catalog: The Dartmouth Online Catalog includes romanized records for East Asian materials from 1984 on. Older East Asian titles are being converted to the new online catalog.

Network/Consortium affiliation:

Member of RLG.

19. DUKE UNIVERSITY

East Asian Collection, William R.Perkins Library
Durham, North Carolina 27706
Tel: (919) 684-5287. FAX: (919) 684-2855.

Kristina Kade Troost, Japanese Studies Bibliographer

Year started: In the 1940s

Hours:

Monday-Thursday: 8:00 am - Midnight
Friday: 8:00 am - 10:00 pm
Saturday: 9:00 am - 10:00 pm
Sunday: 10:00 am - Midnight
Holidays: Thanksgiving, Christmas, and New Year's Days closed

Holdings:

Volumes:
    Chinese: 9,187
    Japanese: 15,082
    Korean: 550
Current serials:
    Chinese: 23
    Japanese: 150
    Korean: 1
Current newspapers:
    Chinese: 4
    Japanese: 4
    Korean: 4

Areas of strength:

The collection is predominately Japanese and has particular strengths in Japanese history, literature, culture, arts, and Buddhism. There are extensive holdings on Meiji Restoration, post-World War II politics and government, and twentieth century labor history. The collection is also noted for its holdings of proletarian literature.

Access:

The library is open to the public. Borrowing privileges are given to university faculty and students, adult residents of Durham County and the Duke community, and visiting scholars with letter of reference.

Interlibrary loan service:

Available to all libraries.

Online cataloging:

East Asian materials are cataloged in the OCLC CJK system.

Catalogs for use of the Collection:

Card Catalogs: East asian card catalogs are maintained.

Network/Consortium affiliation:

Member of TRLN (Triangle Research Libraries Network).

Publications:

Lin, Wen-chouh and Edward Martinique. "Cooperative Library Activities in East Asian Studies Between Duke University and the University of North Carolina at Chapel Hill," *CEAL Bulletin* no. 66 (October 1981): 25-28.

20. FAMILY HISTORY LIBRARY

Asian Collection, Family History Library
The Church of Jesus Christ of Latter-day Saints
35 North West Temple Street
Salt Lake City, Utah 84150
Tel: (801) 240-4750. FAX: (801) 240-5551.

Frederick R. Brady, Senior Asian Cataloger

Year started: 1968

Hours:

Monday: 7:30 am - 6:00 pm
Tuesday-Friday: 7:30 am - 10:00 pm
Saturday: 7:30 am - 5:00 pm

Holdings:

Volumes:
Chinese:	3,133
Japanese:	1,316
Korean:	1,100

Current serials:
Chinese:	4
Japanese:	2
Korean:	1

East Asian microfilm reels and fiche cards: 22,158

Areas of strength:

The library is formerly known as the Genealogical Library. The Asian Collection is strong in Chinese genealogies, local histories, and Ch'ing archives; Japanese emigration records (dating from about 1880 to 1940), mortuary records (kakocho) of certain Buddhist temples, and archives of some major *hans*; and Korean genealogies and local histories.

Access:

The entire library, except the Extra Surveillance/Special collections room, is open to the public. The Granite Mountain Records Vault, where film negatives are stored, is not open to the public, but special visitors can apply for permission to tour the vault.

Books and films may be used, free of charge, at the main library. There is a small fee for borrowing films through the Family History Center system. Materials may not be removed from the premises.

Interlibrary loan service:

Restricted to certain libraries. The library's microfilmed holdings circulate to Family History Centers worldwide.

Online cataloging:

Asian materials are still being cataloged manually, but the cataloging will go online in 1991.

Catalogs for use of the Collection:

Card Catalogs: East Asian card catalogs are maintained, but may be closed in the near future.

Online Catalog: The Family History Library Catalog (FHLC) system produces both comfiche catalogs and CD catalogs. All Asian titles and call numbers are entered online for control, but do not appear in the catalogs. The Asian card catalogs are available on microfilm.

Publications:

Telford, Ted A. *Chinese Genealogies at the Genealogical Society of Utah: An Annotated Bibliography.* Taipei, Taiwan: Ch'eng wen ch'u pan she, 1983.

21. FAR EASTERN RESEARCH LIBRARY

5812 Knox Avenue South
Minneapolis, Minnesota 55419
Tel: (612) 926-6887

Jerome Cavanaugh, Director

Year founded: 1978

Hours:

Open weekdays: 9:00 am - 5:00 pm

Holdings:

Volumes:	
Chinese:	86,775
Japanese:	1,845
Korean:	525
Chinese microfilm reels:	170
Current serials:	
Chinese:	450
Korean:	5
Current newspapers:	
Chinese:	4

Areas of strength:

The collection is predominately Chinese, with emphases on language, literature, history, and bibliography. The collection is strong in Chinese dialectal materials: About 2,000 items of southern and northern Min dialects, Wu area dialects, and Kwangtung area dialects (Cantonese and Hakka). There are over 2,000 Current and non-current Chinese serial titles with about 60,000 issues.

The Japanese collection contains primarily works on China. Holdings in the small Korean collection are on language, literature, and history.

Access:

The library is open to the public. Materials are all for reference use only and can not be checked out.

Interlibrary loan service:

Interlibrary loans are restricted to East Asian libraries, foreign and domestic.

Online cataloging:

East Asian materials are cataloged manually.

Catalogs for use of the Collection:

Card Catalogs: East Asian card catalogs are maintained.

Online Catalog: The library has IBM XT and AT online catalogs for Chinese and Japanese monographs and serials.

22. FREER GALLERY OF ART/
ARTHUR M. SACKLER GALLERY

Library of the Freer Gallery of Art and the
Arthur M. Sackler Gallery, Smithsonian Institution
1050 Independence Avenue, Washington, D.C. 20560
Tel: (202) 357-2091

Lily C.-J. Kecskes, Head Librarian

Year founded: 1923

Hours:

Weekdays: 10:00 am - 5:00 pm
Weekends: Closed

Holdings:

Total East Asian holdings: 25,000 volumes (mainly in Chinese and Japanese).

Areas of strength:

The library's primary mission is to support research in the fields of the arts and cultures of Asia and the turn-of-the-century American painting, and to provide a full range of services to support the exhibition, publication, and public programs of the two museums. Its collection provides comprehensive coverage of art as well as history, language and literature, philosophy and religion of these fields. In earlier years the holdings on Chinese art constituted the largest of the library's collections. Later, many Japanese language books were added. In recent years the library has increasingly acquired materials on South and Southeast Asian art.

Special collections:

The library's special materials include an 800-volume Chinese rare book collection and approximately 300 volumes of Japanese wood-block print books. For archival materials, there are 44 glass negatives of Empress dowager Tz'u-hsi, and the Bishop Collection which contains 10,000 photographic images of archaeological and art materials gathered by Carl Whiting Bishop (a Freer employee) during the 1920-30s on his expeditions to China.

Access:

The library is open to the public, and no appointments are needed except for using materials in the archives and the slide collection.

Interlibrary loan service:

Available to all libraries (xeroxing only, no material circulation).

Online cataloging:

East Asian materials are cataloged in the RLIN CJK system.

Catalogs for use of the Collection:

Card Catalogs: East Asian card catalogs are maintained.

Network/Consortium affiliation:

Special member of RLG and member of the RLG Art and Architecture Program Committee.

Publications:

1. *Dictionary Catalog of the Library of the Freer Gallery of Art.* Boston: G.K. Hall, 1967.

2. *Smithsonian Institution Archival, Manuscript, and Special Collection Resources; a Guide.* Washington, D.C.: Smithsonian Institution, 1988. p. 11-12.

3. *Freer Gallery of Art.* Washington, D.C.: The Gallery of Art, 1983. p. 11.

4. *Arthur M. Sackler Gallery.* Washington, D.C.: The Gallery, 1987. p. 20-21.

23. GEORGETOWN UNIVERSITY

East Asian Collection, P.O. Box 37445
Washington, D.C. 20013
Tel: (202) 687-7541. FAX: (202) 687-1215.

Kay Won Lee, Oriental Materials Specialist

Year started: 1950s

Hours:

Monday-Thursday: 8:30 am - Midnight
Friday: 8:30 am - 10:00 pm
Saturday: 10:00 am - 10:00 pm
Sunday: 11:00 am - 12:00 am

Holdings:

Volumes:	
Chinese:	16,658
Japanese:	15,674
Korean:	1,214
Current serials:	
Chinese:	32
Japanese:	52
Korean:	7
Current newspapers:	
Chinese:	3
Japanese:	1
Korean:	2
East Asian microfilm reels and fiche cards:	376

Areas of strength:

East Asian materials in the humanities and social sciences are collected. Strong areas in the collection are: history, literature, language, and linguistics.

East Asian materials in other collections:

The archives, manuscripts, and rare books division holds correspondence and reports sent from Jesuit Missions in the Far East from

1675 to 1682. The Audio Visual Department maintains audio-visuals on China and Japan, and 450 reels of microfilm on Asia.

Access:

The library is open to the public. Borrowing privileges are given to university faculty and students, alumni, and faculty and graduate students of the Washington area institutions. Others may use the library for a fee ($100.00 per year).

Interlibrary loan services:

Available to all libraries.

Online cataloging:

East Asian materials are cataloged in the general OCLC system in romanization only.

Catalogs for use of the Collection:

Card Catalogs:

East Asian card catalogs are maintained.

Network/Consortium affiliation:

Member of CAPCON (Capital Consortium) and the Washington Research Library Consortium.

24. HARVARD UNIVERSITY

Harvard-Yenching Library, 2 Divinity Avenue
Cambridge, Massachusetts 02138
Tel: (617) 495-3327. FAX: (617) 496-6008.

Eugene W. Wu, Librarian

Year founded: 1928

Hours:

Monday-Friday: 9:00 am - 10:00 pm	Summer:
Saturday: 9:00 am - 5:00 pm	Monday-Saturday:
Sunday: Closed	9:00 am - 5:00 pm

Holdings:

Volumes:
Chinese:	430,102
Japanese:	203,069
Korean:	73,349

Current serials:
Chinese:	1,806
Japanese:	988
Korean:	463

Current newspapers:
Chinese:	163
Japanese:	8
Korean:	15

East Asian microfilm reels and fiche cards: 29,636

Areas of strength:

The library is one of the largest for East Asian research outside Asia. Its core collection consists of publications in the humanities and social sciences on both traditional and modern East Asia. The library maintains a large collection of periodicals and newspapers, current and non-current, in paper copy and on microfilm. Besides CJK materials, the library also has a large collection of Western language materials on East Asia (35,218 volumes and 2,143 microfilm reels and fiche cards) and extensive holdings in Manchu, Mongolian, Tibetan, and Vietnamese, totalling 11,767 volumes and 386 microfilm reels and fiche cards.

Special collections:

The library's special collections include Chinese, Japanese, and Korean rare books and manuscripts; Chinese rubbings; Tibetan and Mongolian *Tripitaka*; and Manchu publications. The Chinese rare books collection consists of 14 Sung, 38 Yuan, 1,277 Ming, and 1,880 early Ch'ing editions. Among the Japanese rare books, the 6,500-volume Petzold Buddhist Collection, which includes approximately 3,000 books published during the Edo period and some 200 manuscripts dating from the 13th centuries, is outstanding. The Korean rare editions include a group of genealogies and government examination rosters from the 17th and 18th centuries. Other unique features in the library's special collections are a group of Nakhi (a minority people in China's Yunnan Province) manuscripts in pictograph script; the archives of the Lingnan University Trustees (a missionary university in Canton originally known as the Canton Christian College), 1884-1952; a photographs and slides collection; collections of personal papers, including those of the late Hu Han-min, an early Kuomintang statesman, the late George A. Fitch, who was for many years associated with the YMCA and other missionary activities in China, and the late Joseph Buttinger, author and Vietnam specialist; and the Tiananmen Archives of the Charles L. and Lois Smith Special Collection on Contemporary China.

East Asian materials in other collections:

The Rubel Asiatic Research Collection of the Fine Arts Library, the library of the John K. Fairbank Center for East Asian Research, and the Law School Library also collect East Asian materials.

Access:

Reading and stack privileges (no loans) are available to those who present proper identification and register at the Public Services Desk. There is no charge for in-house use of the library.

Borrowing privileges are extended to all currently registered Harvard students, university faculty and staff, visiting scholars with Harvard ID cards, and faculty spouses and persons granted the privileges by the Librarian. Others may borrow materials upon payment of a fee. In general, all materials in the open stacks may be borrowed, except for periodicals and reference materials.

Travel grants:

Travel grants of up to $200 each are available to scholars and advanced graduate students in Japanese studies from other institutions outside the Boston metropolitan area to consult the library's Japanese collection for research.   These grants are awarded on a merit basis. Grantees are also provided the privilege of free photocopying of up to 100 sheets.   Applications for the grant, including a brief description of the research topic and an estimated budget, should be submitted to Eugene W. Wu, Librarian of the Harvard-Yenching Library.

Interlibrary loan service:

Available to all libraries.

Online cataloging:

The library began cataloging its Western language materials into the general OCLC database in 1981, and its East Asian materials in the OCLC CJK system in 1989.

Catalogs for use of the collection:

Card Catalogs: East Asian card catalogs are maintained.   The library's Chinese, Japanese, and Korean catalogs have been published in book form and can be consulted in the Catalog Room.   The published catalogs are supplemented by an author/title card catalog for later additions.

Online Catalog: The local online catalog is HOLLIS (Harvard On-line Library Information System), which contains romanized records for Harvard-Yenching Library's East Asian materials cataloged since January 1989.   It also contains complete holdings information on all currently received serials.

Network/consortium affiliation:

Member of OCLC and the East Coast East Asian Library Consortium.

Publications:

1. *Catalogues of the Harvard-Yenching Library. Chinese Catalogue.* New York: Garland Pub., 1986. 39 v.

2. *Catalogues of the Harvard-Yenching Library. Japanese Catalogue.* New York: Garland Pub., 1985. 33 v.

3. *A Classified Catalogue of Korean Books in the Harvard-Yenching Institute Library at Harvard University.* Cambridge, Mass., 1962-1980. 3 v.

4. *Union List of Japanese Periodicals in the East Asian Libraries of Columbia, Harvard, Princeton, and Yale Universities,* second edition, 1989; bilingual.

5. Wu, Eugene W. "Ha-fo ta hsueh Ha-fo Yen-ching t'u shu kuan Chung-kuo ku chi" (Chinese rare books in the Harvard-Yenching Library of Harvard University). In *Ku chi chien ting yu wei hu yen hsi hui chuan chi* (Proceedings of the Workshop on the Authentication and Preservation of Chinese Rare Materials), 341-351. Taipei: Chinese Library Association, 1985.

6. Wu, Eugene W. "Ha-fo Yen-ching t'u shu kuan Chung-kuo fang chih chi ch'i t'a yu kuan tzu liao ts'un ts'ang hsien k'uang" (Current holdings of Chinese local gazetteers and other related materials in the Harvard-Yenching Library), *Han hsueh yen chiu* v. 3, no. 2 (December 1985): 369-378.

7. Lai, John Yung-hsiang. *Catalog of Protestant Missionary Works in Chinese,* Harvard-Yenching Library, Harvard University. Boston: G. K. Hall, 1980.

8. Shen, Chin. "Mei-kuo Ha-fo ta hsueh Yen-ching t'u shu kuan ts'ang Chung-kuo shan pen ku chi chieh shao" (Introduction to the Chinese rare books collection of Harvard-Yenching Library), *Ku chi cheng li ch'u pan ch'ing k'uang chien pao* no 204 (February 1989): 33-38.

9. Oka, Masahiko. "Habado Daigaku Enkyo Toshokan zo Washo Kanryaku mokuroku, 1," (Catalog of Japanese books at the Harvard-Yenching Library of Harvard University) *Chosa Kenkyu Hokoku* no. 11 (March 1990).

10. Harvard-Yenching Institute. *Habado Daigaku Kan-Wa Toshokan Nihon zenshu socho mokuroku* (Catalog of Japanese collectanea at the Harvard-Yenching Library of Harvard University). Cambridge, MA: the Institute, 1954.

11. Chiu, A. K'aiming. "Ha-fo ta hsueh Ha-fo Yen-ching hsueh she t'u shu kuan ts'ang Ming tai lei shu kai shu, Part 1" (Introduction to

reference books of Ming dynasty at the Harvard-Yenching Library of Harvard University, Part 1) *Ch'ing hua hsueh pao* new series, v. 2, no. 2 (June 1961): 94-115.

12. Elisseeff, Serge. "The Chinese-Japanese Library of the Harvard-Yenching." *Harvard Library Bulletin* X (1956): 73-93.

13. *Harvard-Yenching Library Occasional Reference Notes.*

14. *Harvard-Yenching Library Bibliographical Series.*

25. UNIVERSITY OF HAWAII, MANOA

Asia Collection, Hamilton Library, 2550 The Mall
Honolulu, Hawaii 96822
Tel: (808) 956-8116. (808) 956-8042.
FAX: (808) 956-5968.

Lan Hiang Char, Acting Head

Year started: 1920

Hours:

Monday-Thursday: 7:30 am - 11:00 pm
Friday: 7:30 am - 5:00 pm
Saturday: 9:00 am - 5:00 pm
Sunday: 1:00 pm - 10:00 pm

Holdings:

Volumes:
Chinese:	103,008
Japanese:	103,675
Korean:	35,047

Current serials:
Chinese:	906
Japanese:	679
Korean:	232

Current newspapers:
Chinese:	13
Japanese:	5
Korean:	8

East Asian microfilm reels and fiche cards: 13,029

Areas of strength:

The collection has strong holdings in humanities and social sciences. Specific subject strengths lie in these areas:

Chinese Collection: History, literature, language, fine arts, religion (Buddhism, etc.), and philosophy. The collection is especially strong on basic sources dealing with Ch'ing dynasty (1644-1912) history as well as materials on the local history of the southeast coastal provinces, particularly

Taiwan, Kwangtung, and Fukien. The collection also consists of genealogies of the above areas. Its source materials for the studies of the Republican period (1911-1949) include a large collection of scholarly journals and long runs of central government gazettes published during the period.

In literature, the collection includes traditional fiction and drama materials, with thematic studies, commentaries, and related source materials. The holdings on language studies emphasize Chinese dialects and language instructions, mainly Mandarin, Taiwanese, and Cantonese.

In fine arts, the collection includes a complete series of materials on ancient art, selected works of individual artists, catalogs of major museums in China, and extensive materials on calligraphy and paintings.

The collection has also strong holdings on Chinese philosophy which include publications on the historical development of the various schools of thought, particularly Confucianism and Taoism.

The library has recently made efforts to expand its holdings in the areas of economics, social conditions, population, statistics, and other fields in social sciences.

Japanese Collection: The collection emphasizes source materials on the history of the Tokugawa period (1600-1868), modern literature, Buddhism, business, and economics. Its area studies materials are strong on the Ryukyus, Satsuma, and Hokkaido. The collection also includes materials on the performing arts such as *kabuki, no,* and *kyogen.*

Korean Collection: As one of the major Korean resource centers in this country, the Korean collection supports the university's Korean studies program through the development of its bibliographic resources and the acquisition of current publications on history, literature, and economics.

Special collections:

Chinese:

News Clippings on the People's Republic of China (from 1949 to the 1960s) published by the Union Research Institute, Hong Kong. The collection contains 1,034 reels of microfilms covering politics, military affairs, economic conditions, education and culture, and overseas Chinese affairs, with an index.

86 microfilm reels of Tun-huang Buddhist Manuscripts (Tun-huang hsieh ching) made from holdings held by the Peking Library.

Japanese:

The Sakamaki Collection contains over 2,000 volumes mainly on the Ryukyus, collected by University of Hawaii Professor Shunzo Sakamaki. This collection is reportedly the best outside Japan.

The Kajiyama Collection, the personal library of Japanese novelist Toshiyuki Kajiyama, consists of over 7,000 titles including historical documents on Japanese migration and the novelist's personal works.

Korean:

Imanishi Hakushi Shushu Chosenbon: 153 microfilm reels of Dr. Imanishi's collection of Korean historical sources on Sino-Korean relations, originally owned by the Tenri Central Library, Japan.

The Gyujanggag Collection: 475 microfilm reels of archival materials from the Yi Dynasty Royal Library, Korea.

East Asian materials in other collections:

The Center for Chinese Studies recently has been developing a "China Abroad Archives" which includes manuscripts, research papers, and other archival materials contributed by Chinese scholars outside of China; selected materials published by Hawaii-based scholars; and materials on China's 1989 democracy movement such as underground literature, oral history, and video tapes.

The Center for Korean Studies library contains microfilms of retrospective files of Korean newspapers and United States dissertations on Korea.

Access:

The library is open to the public. Borrowing privileges are extended to research fellows and staff of the East-West center; faculty, students, and staff of the University of Hawaii; visiting scholars, and local community members.

Interlibrary loan service:

Available to all libraries.

Online cataloging:

East Asian materials are cataloged in the RLIN CJK system

Catalogs for use of the Collection:

Card Catalogs: East Asian card catalogs are maintained but closed since 1985.

Online Catalog: The local online catalog, CARL, contains records for all the East Asian materials in romanized form.

Network/Consortium affiliation:

Member of RLG.

Publications:

1. *The Chinese in Hawaii: A Checklist of Chinese Materials in the Asia and Hawaiian Collections of the University of Hawaii Library*, by Chau Mun Lau. Honolulu: The Library, 1979.

2. *Current Japanese Serials in the University of Hawaii at Manoa Libraries*, by Katherine Yoshimura. Honolulu: Center for Japanese Studies, School of Hawaiian, Asian, and Pacific Studies, University of Hawaii at Manoa, 1989.

3. *Union List of Current Japanese Serials in Six East Asian Libraries of Western North America* (British Columbia,U.C.-Berkeley, UCLA, Hawaii, Hoover, and Washington), compiled by Mihoko Miki. [Los Angeles]: Western Regional Japanese Library Conference, 1988.

4. Matsui, Masato and Katsumi Shimanaka. *Research Resources on Hokkaido, Sakhalen and the Kuriles at the East West Center Library.* Honolulu: East West Center Library, 1967.

5. Lee, Catherine Y. *Arts of Korea: A Checklist of Books in the Asia Collection of the University of Hawaii Library, June, 1979.* Honolulu: The Library, 1981.

6. ____. *Korea: A Selected Guide to Reference Materials in the Asia Collection of the University of Hawaii Library as of December 1978.* Honolulu: The Library, 1979.

7. ____. *Korean Music: A Checklist of Books in the University of Hawaii Library, June 1982.* Honolulu: Asia Collection, University of Hawaii at Manoa, 1982.

26. HOOVER INSTITUTION

East Asian Collection, Hoover Institution on
War, Revolution and Peace
Stanford, California 94305-2323
Tel: (415) 725-3443. FAX: (415) 723-1687.

Ramon H. Myers, Curator-Scholar

Year started: 1945

Hours:

Weekdays: 8:00 am - 5:00 pm
Weekends: Closed

Holdings:

Volumes:
        Chinese: 198,491
        Japanese: 129,472
Current serials:
        Chinese: 884
        Japanese: 238
Current newspapers:
        Chinese: 44
        Japanese: 11
Chinese and Japanese microfilm reels and fiche cards: 27,666

Areas of strength:

The collection has rich holdings in the areas of war, revolution and peace in East Asia. It is particularly strong in source materials on modern China and Japan, many of which are unique and not preserved elsewhere. Subjects covered are politics, law, economics, public finance, sociology, statistics, education, defense, history, and geography; and, to a lesser degree, language, literature, science and technology (including agriculture and industry), etc. Serial holdings of the collection consist of 6,000 Chinese titles which include many pre-1949 Chinese government documents, statistical reports on commerce, and other periodicals; and about 1,800 Japanese titles which include many left-wing journals of the 1920s and their right-wing counterparts of the 1930s and 1940s.

Special collections:

Rare materials in the collection include:

Chinese:

Rich resources on the Chinese Revolution of 1911 and the history of Chinese Communist Party from 1921-1949.

A collection of oral interview cassette tapes and documents from the China Research Institute of Land Economics of Taipei which contain information about Taiwan's monumental land reform between 1950 and 1953 and its important financial and trade reforms of the 1950s and 1960s.

Two Chinese newspapers covering the years of 1957-1960 and 1972-1975 for Shun-te County, Kwangtung that reveal local conditions in this small part of China during a time when historical materials from China were extremely difficult to get.

Holdings of about one hundred underground magazines and publications that appeared in China in 1979 and early 1980.

The James Hayes collection of rare late 19th- and early 20th-century land deeds, merchant account books, lineage records, and private Chinese association handbooks of Hong Kong.

The collection of Tang-wai Opposition Magazines which contains a number of dissident magazines published during 1975-1986 by dissident groups in Taiwan--the largest such collection outside Taiwan.

Japanese:

The Araki Sadao Collection: Papers of General Araki Sadao (1877-1966), comprising memoirs, diaries, reports, speeches, telegrams, correspondence, etc., dating from the beginning of the century to the mid-1930s. Topics covered include the Japanese politics, the Japanese army, the Soviet Union, and the Shanghai Incident (1932). A checklist is available.

The Tokko Collection: Pre-World War II documents and records regarding left- and right-wing activities, mostly in the 1930s.

The Japanese Archival Collection on Korea: 100,000 pages of important documents from the Japanese Legation in Seoul (1894-1905), the

Japanese Residency-General in Korea (1906-1910), and the Japanese Government-General of Chosen in its first year of operation (1910)--all basic source materials for the study of modern Korea.

The Early Nineteenth Century *Ehon* Collection: 1,963 wood-block print, profusely illustrated storybooks, travel guides, etc. (about 500 titles), published in the late eighteenth and early nineteenth centuries.

East Asian materials in other collections:

The Art and Architecture Library holds over 31,000 East Asian vernacular volumes on art and architecture.

Access:

This library is open to the public who are permitted to enter the reading room and use the reference books, current journals and newspapers, and other materials there.

Under a cooperative program with U.C.-Berkeley, borrowing privileges are given to faculty, staff, students, and registered visiting scholars and researchers of both institutions. Visiting faculty, scholars, and students from other institutions may be given special permissions to use the materials in the library but have no loan privileges.

Travel grants for use of the collection:

The Stanford East Asia National Resource Center (SEANRC) provides annually about five grants of up to $500 to support junior faculty who are normally not in easy reach of East Asian research facilities. The grants are given only to U.S. citizens and permanent residents.

Interlibrary loan service:

Available to all libraries.

Online cataloging:

East Asian materials are cataloged in the RLIN CJK system.

Catalogs for use of the Collection:

Card Catalogs: East Asian card catalogs are maintained. However, the library has stopped to file printed cards in its public catalogs since 1984.

Online Catalog: The local online catalog, SOCRATES, includes Chinese and Japanese records cataloged since 1984. These records are in romanized form only.

Network/Consortium affiliation:

Member of RLG and Western Regional Japanese Library Conference.

Publications:

1. *The Library Catalogs of the Hoover Institution on War, Revolution, and Peace: Catalogs of Chinese (13 v.) and Japanese (7 v.) Collections.* Boston: G. K. Hall, 1969; Supplements, 6 v., 1972-77.

2. Myers, Ramon H. "The East Asian Collection," in *The Library of the Hoover Institution on War, Revolution and Peace*, edited by Peter Duignan. Stanford: Hoover Institution, Stanford University, 1985. p. 67-77.

3. Moffitt, Emiko M. "Hoover Institution's East Asian Collection and Its Bibliographical Services," *CEAL Bulletin* No. 68 (June 1982): 14-19.

4. *Union List of Current Japanese Serials in Six East Asian Libraries of Western North America* (British Columbia, U.C.-Berkeley, UCLA, Hawaii, Hoover, and Washington), compiled by Mihoko Miki. [Los Angeles]: Western Regional Japanese Library Conference, 1988.

5. *A Checklist of Japanese Government Publications: East Asiatic Library, University of California, Berkeley, and East Asian Collection, Hoover Institution, Stanford University* (Kashu Daigaku Bakure-ko oyobi Sutanfuodo Daigaku Shozo Nihon seifu kankobutsu mokuroku), edited by Akifumi Oikawa, Eiji Yutani, and Emiko Mashiko Moffitt. Tokyo: Kinokuniya Shoten, 1987. 2 v.

6. *Hoover Institution Microfilms: Asian Supplement.* Stanford: Hoover Institution Press, 1977.

7. Wu, Eugene W. *Leaders of Twentieth Century China: An Annotated Bibliography of Selected Chinese Biographical Works in the Hoover Library.* Stanford: Stanford University Press, 1956.

8. Checklists of holdings of East Asian Collections at U.C-Berkeley and the Hoover Institution, published jointly:

> *A Checklist of Japanese Company Histories* (1978)
> *A Checklist of Japanese Local Histories* (1978)
> *A Checklist of Japanese Newspapers* (1978)
> *Union List of Chinese Periodicals* (1980)
> *A Checklist of Chinese Local Histories* (1980)
> *A Checklist of Chinese Newspapers* (1986)

27. UNIVERSITY OF ILLINOIS

Asian Library, 325 Library, 1408 West Gregory Drive
Urbana, Illinois 61801
Tel: (217) 333-1501. FAX: (217) 244-0398.

Year founded: 1965

Hours:

Weekdays: 8:00 am to 5:00 pm
Weekends: Closed

Holdings:

Volumes:

Chinese:	115,891
Japanese:	51,570
Korean:	5,279

Current serials:

Chinese:	347
Japanese:	240
Korean:	40

Current newspapers:

Chinese:	6
Japanese:	3
Korean:	2

East Asian microfilm reels and fiche cards: 12,040

Areas of strength:

The library has a comprehensive collection of materials in humanities and social sciences. Strong subject areas include modern Chinese and Japanese history; Chinese and Japanese language, linguistics, and literature; politics and government of China; and sociology and anthropology of Japan.

Special collections:

The Joseph K. Yamagiwa Collection contains 17th and 18th century publications in the fields of Japanese language and literature. (The collection is kept in the Rare Book Room.)

Access:

The library is open to the public. Patrons can apply for stack permits at the Circulation Desk.

Interlibrary loan service:

Available to all libraries.

Online cataloging:

East Asian materials were cataloged in the RLIN CJK system up to 1990; they have since then been cataloged in the OCLC CJK system.

Catalogs for use of the Collection:

Card Catalogs: East Asian card catalogs are maintained.

Online Catalog: The local online catalog, FBR, includes East Asian records in romanized form only.

Network/Consortium affiliation:

Member of OCLC, CIC, and the Lincoln Trail Library System.

Publications:

Wong, William S. "Developing a Chinese-Language Collection: The Illinois Experience," *Illinois Libraries* v.71, no.7 (September 1989): 353-57.

28. INDIANA UNIVERSITY

East Asian Collection, Indiana University Library, E860
Bloomington, Indiana 47405
Tel: (812) 855-9695. FAX: (812) 855-8229.

Thomas H. Lee, East Asian Librarian

Year started: 1961

Hours:

Monday-Thursday: 8:00 am - Midnight
Friday: 8:15 am - 9:00 pm
Saturday: 10:00 am - 9:00 pm
Sunday: 11:00 am - Midnight
Holidays: Closed on Thanksgiving, Christmas, and New Year's Days.

Holdings:

Volumes:	
Chinese:	92,398
Japanese:	31,457
Korean:	6,050
Current serials:	
Chinese:	407
Japanese:	218
Korean:	46
Current newspapers:	
Chinese:	17
Japanese:	4
Korean:	6
East Asian microfilm reels:	1,109

Areas of strength:

East Asian materials in the humanities and social sciences are collected. The Chinese Collection is strong in language and literature, history (especially Ming and Ch'ing dynastic histories), classics and collectanea, religion, philosophy, archaeology, fine arts, communism, and politics and government. The Japanese Collection is strong in pre-modern history and literature (particularly those of the Edo and Meiji periods), fine arts, education, sociology, political science, and economic conditions. The

Korean Collection focuses on language, literature, history, social movements, and reference works.

Special collections:

The microfilm *Ebara Bunko* collection with 3,736 volumes on 207 reels and the Daitokyo Kinen Bunko's *Edo Bungaku Sokwan* collection of 92 microfilm reels contain rare materials on Edo literature and culture. The small rare book collection holds some early Chinese and Japanese works including the manuscript edition of the Ch'ing novel, *Lu yeh hsien tsung* (prefaced by Emperor Ch'ien-lung in 1764), and Japanese translations of Chinese classic novels, *Shinpen Suiko gaden* (1807-1838) and *Gahon Saiyu zenden* (1806-1837), in wood-block editions.

East Asian materials in other collections:

East Asian materials are also collected by the Fine Arts Library, which has 30,000 slides and 1,500 photographs on East Asian subjects; the Archives of Traditional Music which contains 1,407 audio recordings of East Asian music; the Kinsey Institute Library known for its over 100 East Asian vernacular volumes on erotic literature; and the Indiana University Art Museum with over 2,000 Japanese prints of the Ukiyo-e School and about 75 surimonos. In addition, the Charles Boxer Collection, held in the Lilly Library, contains about 100 rare items on Japan during the country's early intercourse with the West (1542-1800), and some Chinese wood-block books printed by the Jesuits in China during the 17th and 18th centuries. The Tibetan Collection (about 5,000 volumes) is housed in the main library.

Access:

The library is open to the public. Borrowing privileges are extended to faculty and students of the university and CIC member institutions. Visiting scholars may check out materials by special arrangements.

Interlibrary loan service:

Available to all libraries.

Online cataloging:

East Asian materials are cataloged in the OCLC CJK system.

Catalogs for use of the collection:

Card catalogs: East Asian card catalogs are maintained.

Online catalog: The local online catalog, IO (Information Online), contains romanized records for East Asian materials cataloged since 1986.

Network/consortium affiliation:

Member of OCLC and CIC.

Publications:

1. *Chinese Serials Holdings of the East Asian Collection, Indiana University Libraries*, 1986.

2. *Japanese Serials of the East Asian Collection, Indiana University Library*, 1987.

3. *Korean Serials of the East Asian Collection, Indiana University Library*, 1989.

29. INSTITUTE FOR ADVANCED STUDIES OF
WORLD RELIGIONS

The Library, Road #2, Route 301
Carmel, New York 10512
Tel: (914) 225-1445; (516) 689-5207.
FAX: (914) 225-1485.

Lena Lee Yang
Library Director and East Asian Librarian

Year founded: 1972

Hours:

Weekdays: 9:00 am - 5:00 pm

Holdings:

The Library collects materials in 32 Asian and 11 non-Asian languages. Its holdings include over 72,000 volumes, 465 current periodical titles, more than 50,000 monographs and manuscripts in microforms, maps, and audio materials.

Areas of strength:

The library offers notable research resources for the study of Buddhism, Hinduism and Indology, Islam, East Asian, South Asian, and Southeast Asian religions. It also has supportive reference works on Asian history, cultural arts, and the comparative study of religions.

The Library is particularly strong in its collection of Buddhist materials which include Chinese, Japanese, and Korean editions of the Chinese Tripitaka; various editions of the Tibetan Kanjur-Tanjur in reprint and/or microform; and the Pali Tripitaka in various Southeast Asian languages.

Special collections:

The C. T. Shen collection of Buddhist canons and Buddhist literature in general; the Richard A. Gard collection of Buddhist and related studies; the Ngiam Hoo-pan collection of Chinese Buddhist texts; the Ming Southern edition of the Chinese Tripitaka (incomplete); the Richard Hu

See-yee Chi collection of Buddhist philosophy and Chinese art; and the Chinese Manuscripts from Tun-huang preserved in the British Museum and the Bibliotheque Nationale (on microfilm).

Access:

In-house use of reference materials is free.   Access to other materials in the closed stacks requires the assistance of library staff. Materials may not be checked out.

Interlibrary loan service:

Available to all libraries. The library will provide microfiche copies or photo copies at minimal cost within copyright law provision.

Online cataloging:

East Asian materials are cataloged in the OCLC CJK system.

Catalogs for use of the Collection:

Card Catalogs: East Asian card catalogs are maintained.

Network/Consortium affiliation:

Member of OCLC; NYATLA (New York Area Theological Library Association); and LILRC (Long Island Library Resource Council).

Publications:

1. *Buddhist Text Information* (BTI), edited by Richard A. Gard; quarterly, 1974-

2. *A Classified Catalogue of Chinese Books in the Library of the Institute for Advanced Studies of World Religions*, compiled by Lena Lee Yang. Stony Brook, N.Y.: The Institute, 1981.

30. UNIVERSITY OF IOWA

Oriental Collection, Library, Iowa City, Iowa 52242
Tel: (319) 335-5884. FAX: (319) 335-5830.

Peter Xinping Zhou, Chinese Studies Librarian
Hideyuki Morimoto, Japanese Studies Librarian

Year started: 1965

Hours:

Monday-Thursday: 7:30 am - 1:00 am
Friday: 7:30 am - 11:00 pm
Saturday: 8:00 am - 11:00 pm
Sunday: 10:00 am - 1:00 am

Holdings:

Volumes:

Chinese:	45,000
Japanese:	25,000
Korean:	200

Current serials:

Chinese:	200
Japanese:	100

Areas of strength:

The collection contains East Asian materials mostly in the humanities. Subject strengths: Chinese and Japanese history, language and literature, and East Asian religion.

Special collections:

The David Middleton Reed Collection (2,600 volumes) contains primary research materials on Chinese civilization.

East Asian materials in other collections:

The Art Library has extensive holdings in East Asian languages on East Asian art.

Access:

The library is open to the public. Borrowing privileges are given to University of Iowa students, staff, and faculty, visiting faculty and scholars, and all residents of Iowa. Special privileges for using the library are granted to faculty of CIC and RLG member institutions.

Interlibrary loan service:

Available to all libraries.

Online cataloging:

East Asian materials are cataloged in the RLIN CJK system.

Catalogs for use of the Collection:

Card Catalogs: East Asian card catalogs are maintained but closed since 1985. Currently romanized shelflist cards are filed in the general shelflist catalog.

Online Catalog: The local online catalog, OASIS, contains East Asian records in romanized form only.

Network/Consortium affiliation:

Member of RLG and CIC.

31. UNIVERSITY OF KANSAS

East Asian Library, Lawrence, Kansas 66045
Tel: (913) 864-4669

Eugene Carvalho, Librarian

Year founded: 1964

Hours:

Monday-Thursday: 8:00 am - Midnight
Friday: 8:00 am - 8:00 pm
Saturday: 10:00 am - 5:00 pm
Sunday: 1:00 pm - Midnight

Holdings:

Volumes:
Chinese:		83,893
Japanese:		46,144
Korean:		1,000

Current serials:
Chinese:		230
Japanese:		161
Korean:		3

Current newspapers:
Chinese:		9
Japanese:		2
Korean:		1

East Asian microfilm reels and fiche cards: 3,500

Areas of strength:

The collection has comprehensive coverage in humanities and social sciences. It is particularly strong in East Asian art history (e.g., Chinese Yuan dynasty painting and Japanese Edo period painting; the Bunjinga and Nanga).

East Asian materials in other collections:

East Asian materials are also held in the Art Library and the Science Library.

Access:

The library is open to the public. The following categories of individuals have borrowing privileges: University of Kansas students, staff and faculty; all residents of the State of Kansas; students, staff, and faculty of other institutions of higher learning located in Kansas; University of Kansas alumni; and friends of the Library. A valid library card must be presented in order to borrow library materials.

Interlibrary loan service:

Available to all libraries.

Online cataloging:

East Asian materials are cataloged in the OCLC CJK system.

Catalogs for use of the Collection:

Card Catalogs: East Asian card catalogs are maintained.

Online Catalog: The local online catalog (generally referred to as the OCAT or LCAT) includes East Asian bibliographic records in Romanized form only.

32. LIBRARY OF CONGRESS

Asian Division, John Adams Building, First Floor
Room A-1024, Washington, D.C. 20540
Tel: (202) 707-5420. FAX: (202) 707-6269.

Warren M. Tsuneishi, Chief
Richard C. Howard, Assistant Chief
Chi Wang, Head, Chinese Section. (202) 707-5423/5425
Hisao Matsumoto, Head, Japanese Section. (202) 707-5430
Key P. Yang, Head, Korean Section. (202) 707-5424

Year founded: 1928

Hours:

Weekdays: 8:30 am - 5:00 pm
Saturdays: 8:30 am - 12:30 pm

Holdings: (as of September 30, 1990)

Volumes:

Chinese:	583,532
Japanese:	730,073
Korean:	99,482

Current serials:

Chinese:	2,359
Japanese:	7,194
Korean:	737

Current newspapers:

Chinese:	43
Japanese:	19
Korean:	12

East Asian microfilm reels and fiche cards: 36,716

Areas of strength:

The Asian Division (known until 1978 as the Orientalia Division) has the largest East Asian collection in North America. Materials held by its Chinese, Japanese, and Korean Sections cover most subjects about the East Asian countries, and are particularly strong in the humanities, social sciences, and law.

The Chinese collection started in 1869, when the Ch'ing Emperor donated ten works in 933 stitch-bound volumes, contained in 130 *tao*, to the United States Government. Today, the collection has grown to cover all the major subject areas of Chinese studies. It is particularly strong in history, literature, law, archaeology, and political science. It covers also quite extensively the natural and applied sciences and some holdings of ancient works on Chinese agriculture, botany, and medicine. Among its rare items are the 4,000 local histories, 41 volumes of the original manuscripts of the encyclopedia *Yung-lo ta tien* (compiled during 1403-1409), and a rare book collection of 2,000 titles including the oldest printed books in the Library of Congress and the some 1,500 imprints of the Ming dynasty (1368-1644). In addition to Chinese materials, the collection contains several thousand volumes in Manchu, Mongolian, Tibetan, and Nakhi languages.

The Japanese collection began in 1875, when the Japanese government accepted a proposal for an exchange of government publications to be housed in the Library of Congress. It represents now the preeminent research and information resource on Japan outside of that country itself. The collection is particularly rich in the humanities, social sciences, science and technology, government publications, and periodicals. Among its unique holdings are printed books and manuscripts that predate the reign of the Emperor Meiji (1868-1912)--about 4,200 titles in some 14,200 fascicles, and runs of approximately 17,000 periodical titles and more than 7,000 reels of microfilm which cover prewar censored materials, publications of the South Manchurian Railway Company, and prewar Japanese-American newspapers published in the United States.

The Korean collection began in the early 1900s and is currently the largest outside of East Asia. It covers all important subjects, ranging from the classics, history, and traditional literature through the arts, social sciences, and natural sciences. The collection is a rich source for North Korean publications and maintains about 338 periodicals and 66 newspapers from North Korea.

Special collections:

Chinese Section:

Notable special collections include the Tun-huang manuscripts collection which includes early Chinese manuscripts dated from the T'ang dynasty (618-907); the Manchu Collection which is the largest such collection in the United States with 400 titles; the Mongolian Collection of rare manuscripts and xylographs; the Tibetan Collection which contains the

Tibetan Tripitaka, sutras of the Kanjur and Tanjur, and other Tibetan manuscripts; and the Nakhi (or Moso) pictographic manuscript collection.

Japanese Section:

Rare materials include the Crosby Stuart Noyes Collection of late 18th and 19th century Japanese illustrated books, prints, and drawings; the South Manchurian Railway Company Collection which contains source materials on Japan's prewar economic and political influence in Manchuria, China, Korea, and Soviet Union; the Kan'ichi Asakawa Collection of materials on Japanese Buddhist sects; the *Hyakumanto dharani* (One Million Prayer Charms) with some printed scrolls dated from 770 A.D.; and the collections of microfilm copies of the Japanese Foreign Office archives and documents of the former Japanese Imperial Army and Navy ministries covering the period of 1868-1945.

Korean Section:

Special materials include the *Yijo sillok* (Annals of the Yi dynasty) in 848 volumes; the collection of Korean books in Chinese in 4,500 volumes including the early editions of the phonological work, *Hunmin chongum* (ca. 1430) and the work on ethics, *Samgang haengsilto* (1432); and the North Korean Collection which contains over 10,000 titles published in North Korea since 1945.

East Asian materials in other collections:

East Asian maps and atlases are held by the Geography and Map Division, which is notable for its special collections such as the Hummel Collection, the Warner Collection, etc. of rare manuscript maps of China, Korea, and Japan.

East Asian legal materials are held by the Far Eastern Law Division (see entry number 33).

Access:

The library is open to the public. There are no on-site borrowing privileges; no loans made to individuals except through interlibrary loan.

Interlibrary loan service:

Available to all libraries.

Online cataloging:

East Asian monographs are cataloged in the RLIN CJK system. East Asian serials are cataloged under the CONSER project in romanization. Both the monographic CJK records and the romanized serials records can be found in OCLC and RLIN.

Catalogs for use of the Collection:

Card Catalogs: East Asian card catalogs are maintained but closed since 1984. In December 1988, LC Cataloging Distribution Service terminated its printing of the CJK catalog cards.

Online Catalog: The local online system, the Library of Congress Information System (LOCIS,) includes the MUMS (Multiple Use MARC System), which contains updated preliminary level CJK records in romanization that have been cataloged since 1984, and the "PREMARC" CJK records cataloged from 1958 to 1983 in romanization but with subject access.

Network/Consortium affiliation:

No formal membership affiliation with consortia/networks, but participates in specific network projects (i.e., RLIN/CJK), and uses network/consortia systems.

Publications:

1. *Far Eastern Languages Catalog.* Detroit: G. K. Hall, 1972. 22 v.

2. *A Catalog of Chinese Local Histories in the Library of Congress*, by Chu Shih-chia. 1942.

3. *A Descriptive Catalogue of Rare Chinese Books in the Library of Congress*, by Wang Chung-min. 1957.

4. *Chinese Periodicals in the Library of Congress*: 1985 edition, by Huang Han-chu and Jen Hseo-chin; 1988 edition, by Huang Han-chu.

5. Hu, Shu Chao. *The Development of the Chinese Collection in the Library of Congress.* Boulder, Colo.: Westview Press, 1979.

6. *The Noyes Collection of Japanese Prints, Drawings, etc., Presented by Crosby Stuart Noyes.* 1906.

7. *Checklist of Archives in the Japanese Ministry of Foreign Affairs, Tokyo, Japan, 1868-1945, Microfilmed for the Library of Congress, 1949-1951,* by Cecil Uyehara. 1954.

8. *Japanese National Government Publications in the Library of Congress,* by Thaddeus Ohta. 1980.

9. *Japanese Local Histories in the Library of Congress: A Bibliography,* by Philip M. Nagao. 1988.

10. *Pre-Meiji Works in the Library of Congress: Japanese Mathematics,* by Shojo Honda. 1982.

11. *The Japanese Collection [of] the Library of Congress* (a folded poster). 1989. Bilingual.

12. Kuroda, Andrew Y. "A History of the Japanese collection in the Library of Congress, 1874-1941," in *Senda Masao Kyoju koki kinen toshokan shiryo ronshu.* Tenri: 1970; p. 281-327.

13. Yang, Key Paik. *Ch'uryoso yokkun Miguk Kakhoe Tosogwan sojang pukkoe charyo mongnokchip* (Selected North Korean source materials held in the Library of Congress). Seoul, Korea: Kukt'o T'ongirwon, 1970.

33. LIBRARY OF CONGRESS

Far Eastern Law Division, Law Library
James Madison Building, LM235, Washington, D.C. 20540
Tel: (202) 707-5085

Tao-tai Hsia, Chief

Year founded: 1954

Hours:

Weekdays: 8:30 am - 4:30 pm
Weekends: Closed
(Note: Most of collection accessible through the Law Reading
Room:
8:30 am - 9:00 pm weekdays, 8:30 am - 5:00 pm Saturday; and 1:00 pm -
5:00 pm Sunday)

Holdings:

Volumes:
Chinese: 27,450
Japanese: 69,570
Korean: 8,785
Current serials:
Chinese: 288
Japanese: 619
Korean: 145
Current newspapers:
Chinese: 2
Japanese: 4
Korean: 3
East Asian microfilm reels and fiche cards: 1,074

Areas of strength:

The Law Library's Asian collections are the most complete outside
of the Far East.   Among the rich resources available through the Far
Eastern Law Division are those used in the study of imperial Chinese law,
including many sets of Ch'ing dynasty works in traditional Chinese bindings.
These are large collections of government gazettes for the late Ch'ing,
Republican and Japanese-occupation periods as well.   The Korean law

collection includes a 29-volume set of original legal classics of the Yi dynasty (1392-1910), some handwritten and others in wood-block print. The division has the archive of Chinese Communist legal documents held by the Bureau of Investigation, Ministry of Justice, Republic of China, entitled *Ssu fa hsing cheng pu tiao ch'a chu so ts'ang Chung kung fa lu wen chien* (28 volumes) and a complete set of the *Horei zensho* (Statutes at large) from Japan on microfilm. This series includes laws enacted from 1968 to 1945.

As part of its collections, the Law Library also holds monographs, gazettes, and other serial publications on the current laws of such countries as Burma, Cambodia, China, Hong Kong, Indonesia, Japan, North Korea, South Korea, Laos, Malaysia, Mongolia, Singapore, Taiwan, Thailand, and Vietnam.

East Asian materials in other collections:

Comprehensive East Asian collections in humanities and social sciences and some ancient Chinese and Japanese legal items are held by the Asian Division (see entry under Library of Congress--ASIAN DIVISION).

Access:

The library is open to the public. Borrowing, other than interlibrary loan, is restricted to Congressional users and Library of Congress staff members.

Interlibrary loan service:

Available to all libraries through Library of Congress Loan Division.

Online cataloging:

East Asian materials are cataloged in the RLIN CJK system.

Catalogs for use of the Collection:

Card Catalogs: Card catalogs for the Division's holdings are maintained. The Library of Congress *Far Eastern Languages Catalog* (G. K. Hall, 1972) contains records of the Division holdings cataloged during 1958-1971.

Online Catalog: The Division has access to the Library of Congress computer catalog systems, MUMS and SCORPIO, which include law and other materials in all languages. In addition, the Division has a database of bibliographic information on articles in English covering Chinese law (1986 to present) in PROCITE format.

Publications:

1. Cho, Sung Yoon. *Japanese Writings on Communist Chinese Law 1946-1974: A Selected Annotated Bibliography.* Washington, D.C.: Library of Congress, 1977.

2. _____. *Law and Legal Literature of North Korea: A Guide.* Washington, D.C.: Library of Congress, 1988.

3. Hsia, Tao-tai. *Guide to Selected Legal Sources of Mainland China: A Listing of Laws and Regulations and Periodical Legal Literature.* Washington, D.C.: Library of Congress, 1967.

4. *Japanese Legal Periodicals: A Checklist of Holdings.*

34. UNIVERSITY OF MARYLAND

East Asia Collection
College Park, Maryland 20742-7011
Tel: (301) 405-9133. FAX: (301) 454-4985.

Frank Joseph Shulman, Curator and Head

Year started: 1963

Hours:*

Weekdays: 10:00 am - 5:00 pm
Saturday: Noon - 5:00 pm

Holding:

Volume:

Chinese:	26,802
Japanese:	40,905
Korean:	4,026

Serials:

Chinese:	625
Japanese:	668
Korean:	126

Newspapers:

Chinese:	11
Japanese:	5
Korean:	2

Areas of strength:

The collection is strong in reference works (9,000 volumes in East Asian and other languages) and periodicals (17,000 volumes in CJK languages) in the humanities and social sciences. Specific subject strengths lie in Chinese and Japanese history and literature.

Special Collections:

The Gordon W. Prange Collection of Publications and Unpublished Materials from the Allied Occupation of Japan (1945-1949) contains over 60,000 monographs, 15,000 periodical titles, and more than 18,000 newspaper titles in Japanese dating from the first half of the Allied

Occupation period.   Altogether they constitute the single most comprehensive collection of Japanese-language imprints from that era found anywhere in the world, Japan included.

East Asian materials in other collections:

Luther Whiting Mason Collection of the Music Educators National Conference Historical Center contains 250 rare items including musical instruments presented to Mason (1828-1896) by Japanese Court Musicians; Japanese art and artifacts; books, papers, photographs, and other documents- -all from the early Meiji period.

Access:

Library is open to all users above high school age.   There are restrictions for circulation of library materials for home use: Borrowing privileges are extended to faculty members, students, and alumni of the university at all campuses of the university system, including the University of Maryland at Baltimore County and the Towson State University. Visiting scholars may apply for borrowing privileges on a case by case basis. Members of the community may use library facilities, but may not borrow library materials.

The East Asia Collection circulates not only monographs but also bound and unbound periodicals (for one week at a time) and reference books (overnight).

Interlibrary loan service:

Available to all libraries.   Bound volumes of periodicals and reference books from the East Asian Collection circulate on interlibrary loan on a case by case basis.

Online cataloging:

East Asian materials are cataloged in the OCLC CJK system.

Catalogs for use of the Collection:

Card Catalogs: East Asian card catalogs are maintained.

Online Catalog: The local online catalog, VICTOR (part of the CARL network), includes East Asian materials cataloged since the late 1980s in romanized form only.

Network/Consortium affiliation:

Member of OCLC.

Publications:

1. *M.A., M.B.A., and M.S. Theses Relating to East, Southeast, and South Asia Accepted by the University of Maryland at College Park Through December 1988*, prepared by Kay L. Dove and Andi S. Giri under the direction of Frank Joseph Shulman. 1990.

2. Shulman, Frank Joseph. *Bibliography on the Allied Occupation of Japan: A Bibliography of Western-Language Publications From the Years 1970-1980* (Preliminary Edition). 1980.

---

*These are the hours while the Collection is temporarily housed at the Hornabake Library. The collection will be open longer and with evening hours after the library's renovation project, which was started in January 1991, is completed.

35. UNIVERSITY OF MICHIGAN

Asia Library, Ann Arbor, Michigan 48109-1205
Tel: (313) 764-0406. FAX: (313) 936-3630.

Weiying Wan, Head

Year founded: 1948

Hours:

Monday-Thursday: 8:00 am - Midnight
Friday: 8:00 am - 10:00 pm
Saturday: 10:00 am - 6:00 pm
Sunday: 1:00 pm - Midnight

Holdings:

Volumes:
Chinese:	262,064
Japanese:	212,130
Korean:	4,118

Current serials:
Chinese:	925
Japanese:	1,207
Korean:	60

Current newspapers:
Chinese:	64
Japanese:	12
Korean:	3

East Asian microfilm reels and fiche cards: 53,402

Areas of strength:

The library has a very strong and comprehensive East Asian vernacular collection on China, Japan, and Korea. Its rich holdings cover all important subjects in humanities and social sciences including anthropology, archaeology, religion, history, language and linguistics, phonology, literature, drama, theater, music, education, ethics, fine arts, geography, economics, business, sociology, journalism, library science, military history and science, communism, and political science.

Special collections:

The library's special materials and collections include: Union Research Institute (Hong Kong) Classified Files on China; Red Guards materials (over 20,000 pieces); the Classified Files on the Great Cultural Revolution compiled by the Contemporary China Research Institute; rare editions of Chinese fiction in Japanese collections; Ming local gazetteers and literary collections; National Peking Library Rare Book Collection on microfilm; British Public Record Office Files on China; Tun-huang materials from Beijing, Taipei, the British Museum, and the Bibliotheque Nationale; Japanese local history; 8,000 scripts of Japanese folk drama; materials on the occupation of Japan; Japanese literature; Japanese Diet Proceedings; Bartlett Collection of old Japanese botanical books, manuscripts, and Materia Medica; and Kamada Collection of Prewar Japanese Works.

East Asian materials in other collections:

The Fine Arts Library has a collection of works on art in Chinese and Japanese.

Access:

The library is open to the public. Borrowing privileges are granted to University of Michigan faculty, students, staff, and faculty of CIC members. Visiting scholars certified by University colleges and departments may also borrow materials.

Travel grants:

The library provides a number of travel grants to help off-campus users defray their travel, lodging and photocopying expenses up to $250.00 per award. Interested applicants may send a letter stating their research projects and the materials they intend to use to the Center for Chinese Studies or the Center for Japanese Studies of the university.

Interlibrary loan service:

Available to all libraries.

Online cataloging:

East Asian materials are cataloged in the RLIN CJK system.

Catalogs for use of the Collection:

Card Catalogs: East Asian card catalogs are maintained but closed since 1989.

Online Catalog: The local online catalog, MIRLYN, contains all CJK records of the Asia Library in romanization.

Network/Consortium affiliation:

Member of RLG, CIC, and the Midwest Library Consortium (with the University of Chicago).

Publications:

1. *Catalogs of the Asia Library, University of Michigan.* Boston: G. K. Hall, 1978. 25 v.

2. Ma, Wei-yi. *A Bibliography of Chinese-language Materials on the People's Communes.* Ann Arbor: Center for Chinese Studies, University of Michigan, 1982.

3. *A Checklist of Chinese Local Gazetteers in Asia Library*, 1968.

4. Fukuda, Naomi. "Japanese Collection at the University of Michigan," *Inforasia* v. 1, no. 2 (April/June 1974): 1-9.

36. UNIVERSITY OF MINNESOTA

East Asian Library, S-75 Wilson Library
Minneapolis, Minnesota 55455
Tel: (612) 624-9833

Yuan Zhou, East Asian Librarian

Year started: 1965

Hours:

Monday, Wednesday-Friday: 9:00 am - 5:00 pm
Tuesday: 9:00 am - 8:00 pm
Saturday: 1:00 pm - 5:00 pm
Sunday: Closed

Holdings:

Volumes:
       Chinese: 61,500
       Japanese: 32,419
Current serials:
       Chinese: 290
       Japanese: 170
       Korean: 7
Current newspapers:
       Chinese: 10
       Japanese: 3
       Korean: 4
East Asian microfilm reels and fiche cards: 1,064

Areas of strength:

The collection contains materials primarily in humanities and social sciences. Strong subject areas are:

Chinese: Classics, philology, history (especially history of the Ming dynasty), literature, art, philosophy, and religion.

Japanese: History and literature.

The library's special materials include a block-print edition of the Neo-Confucian compendium, *Hsing li ta ch'uan*, dated 1415.

East Asian materials in other collections:

The Law and Architecture Libraries hold some materials in East Asian languages.

Access:

The library is open to the public. Borrowing privileges are given to university faculty and staff with ID; students with ID and fee statement; and others with a special privilege card or with an alumni card.

Interlibrary loan service:

Available to all libraries.

Online cataloging:

East Asian materials are cataloged in the RLIN CJK system.

Catalogs for use of the Collection:

Card Catalogs: East Asian card catalogs are maintained.

Online Catalog: The local online catalog, LUMINA, includes romanized records for all East Asian monographs and serials cataloged since 1983 (currently about 10,000 titles out of a total of about 30,000). These materials only have shelf list and title cards filed in the card catalogs.

Network/Consortium affiliation:

Member of RLG and CIC.

37. NEW YORK PUBLIC LIBRARY

Oriental Division, Fifth Avenue and 42nd Street
New York, New York 10018
Tel: (212) 930-0721. FAX: (212) 643-0832.

John M. Lundquist, The Susan and Douglas Dillon Chief Librarian

Year founded: 1897

Hours:

Monday, Wednesday, and Friday: 10:00 am - 5:45 pm
Tuesday: 10:00 - 8:45
Saturday: 10:00 am - 5:45 pm
(Note: The Division is closed on Thursdays but service is available
in the main reading room--Room 315).

Holdings:

Volumes:
Chinese:	50,000
Japanese:	48,300
Korean:	21,700

Current serials:
Chinese:	600
Japanese:	350
Korean:	130

Current newspapers:
Chinese:	13
Japanese:	5
Korean:	2

East Asian microfilm reels and fiche cards: 3,700

Areas of strength:

The Division's Chinese collection contains materials in humanities
and social sciences, with special emphases on archaeology, history, religion,
philosophy, dance, literature, language, performing arts, minorities, and
regional studies of Sinkiang, Kansu, Kwangsi, Kweichow, and Tibet. The
collection has rich holdings of Manchu and Tibetan materials.

The Japanese collection concentrates mainly on major subjects in humanities. It was the primary responsible collection in RLG for Japanese technical and scientific journals before 1988. Since 1987 the Division has been collecting Japanese excavation reports comprehensively.

The Korean collection has materials in humanities and some holdings of Korean newspapers published in the United States between 1920-1940.

Special collections:

The Chinese collection has more than 150 rare books and the personal collection of James Legge which contains Ming and Ch'ing dynasty rare books and handwritten manuscripts. The Division also owns the donated personal collections of such China scholars as C. Martin Wilbur, John Watt, and Maud Russell.

East Asian materials in other collections:

The Spencer Collection contains Japanese ukiyo-e and Nara *ehon* and some rare wood-block Chinese books. The Performing Art Collection has East Asian movies, music, books on dance and theater, etc. The Manuscripts Department owns one volume of the original handwritten *Yung-lo ta tien* (dated about 1562), which has not been reprinted by any publisher.

Access:

The library is open to all users free of charge. Books are to be used only on the premises.

Interlibrary loan service:

Available to all libraries.

Online cataloging:

East Asian materials are cataloged in the RLIN CJK system.

Catalogs for use of the Collection:

Card Catalogs: The library's card catalogs were closed in 1971. Since then only shelflist cards are maintained.

Online Catalog: The local online catalog, CATNIP, includes East Asian records in romanized form only.

Network/Consortium affiliation:

Member of RLG and the East Coast East Asian Library Consortium (with Columbia, Cornell, Harvard, Princeton, and Yale for Chinese materials).

Publications:

1. *Dictionary Catalog of the Oriental Collection, New York Public Library.* Boston: G. K. Hall, 1960. 16 v. Supplements, 1976.

2. *Bibliographic Guide to East Asian Studies*, New York Public Library, 1989, including materials cataloged between September 1, 1988 and August 31, 1989.

38. UNIVERSITY OF NORTH CAROLINA

East Asian Collection, CB#3918, Davis Library
Chapel Hill, North Carolina 27599-3918
Tel: (919) 962-1278. FAX: (919) 962-0484.

Edward Martinique, East Asian Bibliographer

Year started: 1964

Hours:

Weekdays: 8:00 am - 11:00 pm   Saturday:
Saturday: 8:00 am - 5:00 pm   10:00 am - 5:00 pm
Sunday: 2:00 pm - 11:00 pm
Intersessions:
Monday-Friday: 8:00 am - 5:00 pm

Holdings:

Volumes:
    Chinese: 80,665
    Japanese: 3,732
    Korean: 247
Current serials:
    Chinese: 543
    Japanese: 84
    Korean: 4
Current newspapers:
    Chinese: 14
    Japanese: 1
    Korean: 2
East Asian microfilm reels and fiche cards: 6,789

Areas of strength:

The collection concentrates on China and Chinese-language publications in humanities. They are shelved together with other language materials in the main library. The strong areas are in history and literature. In history, the emphasis is on the Ming, Ch'ing, and modern era, with rich holdings of archival titles published in Taiwan. In literature, there is a strong collection of secondary works on authors such as Tu Fu and Lu Hsun, and a selection of representative works by and about authors, periods, etc. in general. These are supplemented with a small amount of Japanese sinological works. Japanese-language works in the collection are mostly fiction.

Special collections:

The T. Elbert Clemmons Collection for Oriental Studies was collected with endowed fund that began in 1972. The emphasis of the collection is on the Chinese subject areas such as language, literature, history, philosophy, religion, social sciences, and bibliography, with some works in Chinese.

Access:

The library is open to the public. Borrowing privileges are given to faculty, students, and staff of the three universities in the Triangle area (University of Carolina at Chapel Hill, Duke University, and North Carolina State University), members of the Friends of the Library, and others with special arrangements.

Interlibrary loan service:

Available to all libraries. A special arrangement allows bound serials to be checked out for six months by faculty and graduate students at neighboring Duke University and North Carolina State University.

Online cataloging:

East Asian materials are cataloged in the OCLC CJK system.

Catalogs for use of the Collection:

Card Catalogs: East Asian card catalogs are maintained.

Online Catalog: The local online catalog, BIS (Bibliographic Information System), includes only CJK serials records in romanized form.

Network/Consortium affiliation:

Member of OCLC and SOLINET (Southern Libraries Network).

Publications:

1. *A Decade of the T. Elbert Clemmons Collection of Orientalia.* Chapel Hill, NC: University Printing Service, 1985.

2. "Chinese and Japanese Periodical Holdings in the University of North Carolina at Chapel Hill." Compiled by Amy Lan-Huei Lee. Distributed by the Academic Affairs Library, UNC-CH, Collection Development Department, East Asian Resources, 1989.

3. Martinique, Edward. "The East Asian Collection at the University of North Carolina at Chapel Hill: a Description of Its Contents Using a Sampling Technique," *CEAL Bulletin* no. 61 (February 1980): 41-49.

4. Lin, Wen-chouh and Edward Martinique. "Cooperative Library Activities in East Asian Studies Between Duke University and the University of North Carolina at Chapel Hill," *CEAL BULLETIN* no. 66 (October 1981): 25-28.

39. OBERLIN COLLEGE

East Asian Collection, Oberlin College Library
Seeley G. Mudd Learning Center,
Oberlin, Ohio 44074-1532
Tel: (216) 775-8285. FAX: (216) 775-8886.

Jiann I. Lin, East Asian Specialist

Year started: 1965

Hours:

Weekdays: 8:00 am - 11:00 pm
Saturday: 9:00 am - 11:00 pm
Sunday: Noon - 11:00 pm

Holdings:

Volumes:
    Chinese: 16,221
    Japanese: 706
Current serials:
    Chinese: 103
    Japanese: 10
Current newspapers:
    Chinese: 4
    Japanese: 2

Areas of strength:

This is a collection of Chinese and Japanese materials in humanities and social sciences. Strong subject areas are:

Chinese: Language, literature (20th century), history, political economy, social sciences, philosophy, religion, art, and reference works.

Japanese: Language, literature (modern), history (modern), religion (Buddhism), and art.

Special collections:

The John A. Lacey Collection on Ming dynasty history, and the Homer Dubs (Oxford, England) Collection on pre-modern Chinese history.

East Asian materials in other collections:

The Art Library of the Art Museum contains works of art in Chinese and Japanese.

Access:

The library is open to the public. It is part of NEOMARL (Northeast Ohio Major Academic and Research Libraries). Borrowing privileges are given to Oberlin College faculty, students, and staff. Community people (of the City of Oberlin and the Lorain County) may check out materials after obtaining a library ID card. Some local Oberlin High School students taking courses at the Oberlin College are issued special student college ID for using the library. Others need special permissions for borrowing materials.

Interlibrary loan service:

Available to all libraries.

Online cataloging:

East Asian materials are cataloged in the OCLC CJK system.

Catalogs for use of the Collection:

Card Catalogs: East Asian card catalogs are maintained.

Online Catalog: The local online catalog, OBIS (Oberlin Bibliographic Information System), includes romanized records for East Asian materials cataloged since 1987.

Network/Consortium affiliation:

Member of OCLC, the Northeast Ohio Major Academic Libraries Consortium, and the Cleveland Area Metropolitan Library System.

40. OHIO STATE UNIVERSITY

East Asian Collection, University Libraries
1858 Neil Avenue Mall, Columbus, Ohio 43210-1286
Tel: (614) 292-3502. FAX: (614) 292-3061.

Maureen H. Donovan, Japanese Studies Librarian
Daphne C. Hsueh, Acting Chinese Studies Librarian

Year started: 1962

Hours:

Monday-Saturday: 7:45 am - Midnight
Sunday: 11:00 am - Midnight

Holdings:

Volumes:
Chinese:	88,318
Japanese:	46,175
Korean:	1,125

Current serials:
Chinese:	539
Japanese:	447
Korean:	40

Current newspapers:
Chinese:	20
Japanese:	5
Korean:	5

East Asian microfilm reels and fiche cards: 12,251

Areas of strength:

Chinese: The library collects selectively but systematically in the general humanities; some areas in social sciences including political science, sociology, anthropology and education; but does not collect in the areas of science. The collection is strong in Chinese linguistics (all aspects), and Chinese history (especially local gazetteers).

Japanese: The collection has rich holdings in history, modern Japanese literature, Japanese government white papers and yearbooks, history of science and medicine in Japan, and Japanese company histories.

Ongoing collection development focuses on general reference, philosophy, religion, history, geography, linguistics, literature, political science, sociology/anthropology, economics, and art history.

Special collections:

Leon K. Walters Collection of works on Okinawa.

Access:

The library is open to the public. Borrowing privileges are granted to Ohio State University faculty, staff and students; and faculty of CIC member institutions. Faculty at various local, regional and state colleges and universities are able to get borrowing privileges. Others may borrow materials from the library through other categories of borrowing arrangements.

Interlibrary loan service:

Available to all libraries.

Online cataloging:

East Asian materials are cataloged in the OCLC CJK system.

Catalogs for use of the Collection:

Card Catalogs: Card catalogs are maintained for Chinese collections only.

Online Catalog: The local online catalog, LCS, includes romanized records for CJK materials.

Network/Consortium affiliation:

Member of OCLC, CIC, and Ohionet.

41. UNIVERSITY OF OREGON

Orientalia Collection, Knight Library
Eugene, Oregon 97403
Tel: (503) 686-3096. FAX: (503) 686-3094.

Robert Felsing, Orientalia Bibliographer

Year started: 1967

Hours:

Weekdays: 8:00 am - 11:00 pm	Monday - Friday:
Saturday: 9:00 am - 11:00 pm	8:00 am - 9:00 pm
Sunday: 10:00 - 11:00 pm	Saturday: 9:00 am - 9:00 pm
Summer and intersessions:	Sunday: Noon - 9:00 pm

Holdings:

Volumes:		
	Chinese:	37,160
	Japanese:	36,964
	Korean:	112
Current serials:		
	Chinese:	264
	Japanese:	148
	Korean:	4
Current newspapers:		
	Chinese:	2
	Japanese:	1
	Korean:	1
East Asian microfilm reels and fiche cards:		253

Areas of strength:

Materials in the collection are mainly in Chinese and Japanese, and cover the major subjects in the humanities and social sciences with emphasis on the modern periods. The Chinese collection maintains strengths in modern fiction, art history, and in Ch'ing dynasty and post-imperial history. For local histories, there is a growing collection of materials relating to Fukien Province. The Japanese collection maintains strengths in Buddhism and religion, Taisho and Showa history, modern literature, and language pedagogy. There are strong holdings on the Shirakabaha (White Birch School) literature.

East Asian materials in other collections:

The Architecture and Allied Arts Library presently holds of 1,000 volumes of Japanese and Chinese art history materials.

Access:

The library is open to the public. Borrowing privileges are given to university faculty, students, and staff; and scholars from other OCLC libraries through reciprocal agreement. For others, cards permitting borrowing can be purchased.

Interlibrary loan service:

Available to all libraries.

Online cataloging:

East Asian materials are cataloged in the OCLC CJK system.

Catalogs for use of the Collection:

Card Catalogs: East Asian card catalogs are maintained.

Online Catalog: The collection uses Janus online catalog for East Asian records, supplied by Innovative Interfaces, Inc.

Network/Consortium affiliation:

Member of OCLC.

42. UNIVERSITY OF PENNSYLVANIA

East Asia Collection, Van Pelt Library
34th and Walnut Streets
Philadelphia, Pennsylvania 19104
Tel: (215) 898-3205. FAX: (215) 898-0559.

Karl Kahler, Head

Year started: 1938

Hours:

Monday-Thursday: 8:45 am - Midnight
Friday: 8:45 am - 10:00 pm
Saturday: 10:00 am - 8:00 pm
Sunday: Noon - Midnight

Holdings:

Volume:
Chinese:	75,000
Japanese:	30,000
Korean:	5,000

Current serials:
Chinese:	114
Japanese:	74
Korean:	15

Current newspapers:
Chinese:	5
Japanese:	2
Korean:	3

Chinese and Japanese microfilm reels and fiche cards: 2,152

Areas of strength:

The Collection contains books and journals in Chinese, Japanese, and Korean in the humanities and social sciences on both undergraduate and graduate levels. Its strengths are in language, literature, history, Buddhism, East Asian Civilization 1000-1700, etc.

East Asian materials in other collections:

The University of Pennsylvania Museum Library and Fine Arts Library hold East Asian materials on art and archaeology.

Access:

During the week, the collection is open to everyone with an ID. On weekends, it is restricted to holders of Pennsylvania IDs and members of RLG libraries and selected Philadelphia-area colleges.

Borrowing privileges are restricted to the University of Pennsylvania faculty, students, and staff.   Others may borrow only after special arrangements are made on an individual basis.

Interlibrary loan service:

Available to all libraries.

Online cataloging:

East Asian materials are cataloged in the RLIN CJK system.

Catalogs for use of the Collection:

Card Catalogs: East Asian card catalogs are maintained.

Online Catalog: The local online catalog, Franklin, contains records for East Asian materials in romanized form only.

Network/Consortium affiliation:

Member of RLG.

43. UNIVERSITY OF PITTSBURGH

East Asian Library, 234 Hillman Library
Pittsburgh, Pennsylvania 15260
Tel: (412) 648-8184. FAX: (412) 648-1245.

Thomas C. Kuo, Curator

Year founded: 1961

Hours:

Weekdays: 7:50 am - Midnight
Weekends: 9:00 am - 7:00 pm

Holdings:

Volume:

Chinese:	118,074
Japanese:	28,291
Korean:	1,229

Current serials:

Chinese:	757
Japanese:	175
Korean:	8

Current newspapers:

Chinese:	120
Japanese:	9
Korean:	3

Chinese and Japanese microfilm reels and fiche cards: 4,188

Areas of strength:

The East Asian Library supports the teaching and research activities of the University of Pittsburgh's East Asian Studies Program, which includes almost all subjects in the humanities and social sciences.

The Chinese collection is strong on archaeology/anthropology, language, literature, history (many historical documents and local histories), politics and government, etc. Special materials in the collection include almost all available materials on Taiwan, and 798 volumes of *Wen shih tzu liao* (historical source materials on modern China). The strengths of the Japanese collection lie in language, literature, history, sociology, and economics.

Special collections:

The Chinese rare book collection contains 6 Ming edition titles in 126 volumes.

Access:

The library is open to the public. There is no restriction on the use of the collection within the Library. However, only university faculty members and students with IDs have borrowing privileges. Faculty members of other colleges and universities may apply for special guest cards for checking out materials.

Interlibrary loan service:

Available to all libraries.

Online cataloging:

East Asian materials are cataloged in the OCLC CJK system.

Catalogs for use of the Collection:

Card Catalogs: East Asian card catalogs are maintained.

Networks/Consortium affiliation:

Member of OCLC and Pittsburgh Regional Library Center.

Publications:

1. *Periodicals and Serials of the East Asian Library.* Pittsburgh: University of Pittsburgh Libraries, 1968.

2. *Chinese Local History: A descriptive Holding List.* Pittsburgh: University of Pittsburgh Libraries, 1969.

3. *East Asian Periodicals and Serials: A descriptive Bibliography.* Pittsburgh: University of Pittsburgh Libraries, 1970.

4. *Catalog of Microfilms of the East Asian Library of the University of Pittsburgh.* Pittsburgh: University of Pittsburgh Libraries, 1971.

5. *A Brief Guide to the Use of the East Asian Library*, 1983.

44. PRINCETON UNIVERSITY

Gest Oriental Library and East Asian Collections
Princeton, New Jersey 08544
Tel: (609) 258-3183. FAX: (609) 258-4105.

Antony Marr, Curator

Year started: 1926

Hours:

Weekdays: 9:00 am - 11:00 pm	Summer and intersessions:
Saturday: 10:00 am - 5:00 pm	8:45 am - 4:30 pm
Sunday: 2:00 pm - 11:00 pm	(weekdays)

Holdings:

Volume:
- Chinese: 296,528
- Japanese: 110,880
- Korean: 9,579

Current serials:
- Chinese: 1,350
- Japanese: 1,014
- Korean: 59

Current newspapers:
- Chinese: 11
- Japanese: 4
- Korean: 2

East Asian microfilm reels and fiche cards: 25,134

Areas of strength:

The general collection at Gest Library emphasizes vernacular works on literature and history, with less emphasis placed on the social sciences. The Chinese collection, which forms the core of the Gest Library holdings, encompasses all areas of scholarship but is most comprehensive in traditional literature and history, with strong holdings in philosophy, religion, Buddhism, geography, and the classics. Of special note is the collection on traditional Chinese medicine, which also includes contemporary works on acupuncture and materia medica. Major works in the collection include *Ssu pu ts'ung k'an*, *Ts'ung shu chi ch'eng*, *Ssu k'u ch'uan shu*, and an imperial edition of the *Ku chin t'u shu chi ch'eng*.

The Japanese collection covers similar subject areas with strong holdings in pre-modern and modern history and literature and Japanese sinology.

Holdings in the Korean language cover all academic fields, with historical sources and reference works comprising the outstanding parts of this collection. Of particular note are the Korean Tripitaka, which the Gest Library holds in its entirety, and the *Choson wangjo sillok* (Annals of the Yi dynasty).

The Gest collection also holds books and manuscripts in Manchu, Mongolian, and Tibetan.

Special collections:

The Gest Library was originally begun with the acquisition of many rare books. Today, its rare book collection is one of the most outstanding in the world. The rare book collection houses one hundred two thousand volumes of string-bound books in Chinese. Most of these books were printed in the Ming (1368-1644) and early Ch'ing (1644-1911) dynasties, while many are from earlier periods. The collection covers all aspects of Chinese culture, but is very strong in medicine, Buddhism, history and literature. Some items unique to the collection include a draft manuscript of the dictionary *P'ei wen yun fu*, dated from before 1711; a 1544 edition of Ssu-ma Kuang's historical volume entitled, *Tzu chih t'ung chien*; the manuscript copy of the Ming Veritable Records, *Ta ming shih lu*; a Ming manuscript of *Ch'ang-li wen shih*, Han Yu's literary work; a 1529 edition of the literary anthology *Wen hsuan*; and a five thousand volume compilation of the Buddhist canon *Chi-sha Ta tsang ching*, portions of which date from the Sung (960-1279) and Yuan (1271-1368) Dynasties. The library has also a collection of folk literature, *mu-yu-shu* (about 200 items).

The Rare Book Room also contains some Japanese and Korean works, including the Robinson Go Collection, a set of Japanese books donated by the American Go Association; Manchu, Mongolian and Tibetan language books; Western language books on China, including the Hellmut Wilhelm Collection, and some important memorabilia of Sir Aurel Stein; Captain Leroy Lansing Jane's materials, and numerous curios.

East Asian materials in other collections:

The Marquand Library holds some Chinese and Japanese titles on art history.

Access:

The Collection is open to the public over the age of 16. During evening hours and over weekends, all patrons must sign in and show some form of identification.

For on-site borrowing privilege, patrons must have the Princeton University ID card. Patron without such an ID must show a borrower's card which can be purchased at the main Firestone Library's access office. Princeton Theological Seminary, Institute of Advanced Study and Westminster Choir College borrowers are permitted to use their own institutions ID cards to check out materials, but the ID must bear a Princeton University library barcode obtained from the circulation desk at the Firestone Library.

Travel grants:

Travel grants, usually $250.00 per request, are awarded for out-of-state users of the Gest Library. A letter indicating the reasons why the Gest Library and East Asian Collection are necessary to the scholarly work of the individual should be sent to the library. Requests will then be forwarded to the Program Director of the East Asian Studies Department for approval. After approval, awards will be sent to the applicants.

Interlibrary loan service:

Interlibrary Loan Service is restricted to those libraries affiliated with RLG, and also those which are members of the American Library Association.

Online cataloging:

East Asian materials are cataloged in the RLIN CJK system.

Catalogs for use of the Collection:

Card Catalogs: East Asian card catalogs are maintained.

Online Catalog: The local online catalog contains records for East Asian materials cataloged since January 1, 1980 in romanized form only.

Network/Consortium affiliation:

Member of RLG and the East Coast East Asian Library Consortium.

Publications:

1. Ch'u, Wan-li. *P'u-lin-ssu-tun ta hsueh Ko-ssu-te tung fang t'u shu kuan Chung wen shan pen shu chih* (A Catalogue of the Chinese Rare Books in the Gest Collection of the Princeton University Library). Taipei: Lien ching ch'u pan shih yeh kung ssu, 1984.

2. Hu, Shih. *The Gest Oriental Library at Princeton University.* A reprint from the *Princeton University Chronicle*, V. XV, Spring 1954.

3. Tung, Shih-kang. "The Gest Oriental Library," *CEAL Newsletter* no. 45 (November 1974): 46-49.

4. ____. *Chinese Microfilms in Princeton University: A Checklist of the Gest Oriental Library.* Washington: Center for Chinese Research Materials, Association of Research Libraries, 1969.

5. *Union List of Japanese Periodicals in the East Asian Libraries of Columbia, Harvard, Princeton, and Yale Universities*, second edition, 1989; bilingual.

45. UNIVERSITY OF ROCHESTER

Asia Library, Rochester, New York 14627
Tel: (716) 275-4489

Datta S. Kharbas, Head

Year founded: 1965

Hours:

Weekdays: 9:00 am - Noon; 1:00 pm - 5:00 pm
Weekends: Closed

Holding:

Volume:
Chinese:	28,000
Japanese:	14,000

Current serials:
Chinese:	80
Japanese:	60
Korean:	1

Current newspapers:
Chinese:	5
Japanese:	1

Areas of strength:

The Chinese collection is strong in history, literature, and economics. The Japanese collection has significant strengths in economics, political history, and literature.

Access:

The library is open to the public. Faculty and graduate students from the Rochester Regional Library Council member schools can borrow materials. Scholars from other institutions may apply for special borrowing permissions.

Interlibrary loan service:

Available to all libraries.

Online cataloging:

Asia Library is still doing manual cataloging.

Catalogs for use of the Collection:

East Asian card catalogs are maintained.

Publications:

Catalog of East Asian Collection, 1968. Supplements.

46. ROYAL ONTARIO MUSEUM

H.H. Mu Library, (Far Eastern Library)
Royal Ontario Museum, 100 Queen's Park
Toronto, Ontario M4E 1P3, CANADA
Tel: (416) 586-5718. FAX: (416) 586-5862.

Jack Howard, Librarian

Year founded: 1933

Hours:

Tuesday-Thursday: 1:00 pm - 5:00 pm
Friday: 10:30 am - 4:30 pm
Weekends: Closed

Holdings:

East Asian holdings are about 30,000 volumes (monographs and bound periodicals).

Areas of strength:

The Far Eastern Library is the leading library for Asian art and archaeology in Canada. The library's art and archaeology holdings cover such areas as (in order of strengths) China, Japan, India, Korea, Southeast Asia, and Central Asia.

Special collections:

The library has some Chinese and Japanese rare books and a collection of post-World War II Japanese theater programs (about 30 linear feet).

East Asian materials in other collections:

This library collects mainly in art and archaeology, while the East Asian Library of the University of Toronto collects in literature, history, and social sciences, with some art (see entry under University of Toronto about that library). The two collections, which are within walking distance, complement each other.

Access:

The library is open to the public as a non-lending research library. Borrowing privileges are given to museum staff, University of Toronto faculty and museum studies students, and certain others at the librarian's discretion.

Interlibrary loan service:

Available to all libraries.

Online cataloging:

East Asian materials are cataloged in UTLAS in romanization.

Catalogs for use of the Collection:

Card Catalogs: East Asian card catalogs are maintained.

Online Catalog: The Librarian is using Bibbase (Vendor: Library Technologies, 1142E Bradfield Road, Abington, PA 19001) combined with China Star (JHL Research, 2552 W. Woodland Dr., Anaheim, CA 92801) to produce both CJK/roman cards and in-house online database with displays of CJK scripts.

Network/Consortium affiliation:

Member of UTLAS and the University of Toronto Union of Campus Libraries.

47. RUTGERS STATE UNIVERSITY

East Asian Library, New Brunswick, New Jersey 08903
Tel: (908) 932-7161. FAX: (908) 932-6808.

Nelson Ling-sun Chou, Librarian

Year founded: 1970

Hours:

Monday-Thursday: 8:00 am - Midnight
Friday: 8:00 am - 10:00 pm
Saturday: 10:00 am - 8:00 pm
Sunday: 11:00 am - Midnight

Holdings:

Volume:
Chinese:	92,731
Japanese:	3,632
Korean:	787

Current serials:
Chinese:	206
Japanese:	17
Korean:	17

Current newspapers:
Chinese:	6
Japanese:	2
Korean:	1

East Asian microfilm reels and fiche cards: 3,104

Areas of strength:

The collection is strong in Chinese literature (especially fiction and drama), language, history (especially local histories), and religion (Buddhism).

Special collections:

The microfilm collection of rare books of the National Central Library in Taipei, Taiwan (Series 1-7), and *Ssu k'u ch'uan shu*, chi pu

(Reprint edition by the National Palace Museum in Taipei). A collection of about ninety items of folk literature, *mu-yu-shu*.

Access:

The library is open to the public. Borrowing privileges are given to faculty, staff, and students of the university. Through Friends of the Library, others may obtain borrowing permissions by paying an annual membership fee of $30.00.

Interlibrary loan service:

Available to all libraries.

Online cataloging:

East Asian materials are cataloged in the RLIN CJK system.

Catalogs for use of the Collection:

Card Catalogs: East Asian card catalogs are maintained.

Online Catalog: The local online catalog, IRIS, contains records for East Asian materials in romanized form only.

Network/Consortium affiliation:

Member of RLG.

Publications:

Chinese Periodicals in the East Asian Library. New Brunswick: Rutgers State University, 1973.

48. UNIVERSITY OF SOUTHERN CALIFORNIA

East Asian Library, University Library, University Park
Los Angeles, California 90089-0182
Tel: (213) 740-1772. FAX: (213) 749-1221.

Kenneth Klein, Head

Year founded: 1956

Hours:

Monday-Thursday: 8:00 am - Midnight
Friday: 8:00 am - 5:00 pm
Saturday: 9:00 am - 10 pm
Sunday: 1:00 pm - Midnight
Holidays: 9:00 am - 5:00 pm
Summer: Monday-Thursday: 8:00 am - 8:00 pm
Friday: 8:00 am - 5:00 pm
Saturday: 9:00 am - 5:00 pm

Holdings:

Volume:	
Chinese:	25,198
Japanese:	12,670
Korean:	14,329
Current serials:	
Chinese:	145
Japanese:	84
Korean:	96
Current newspapers:	
Chinese:	9
Japanese:	4
Korean:	6
East Asian microfilm reels and fiche cards:	1,908

Areas of strength:

The East Asian Library collects Chinese, Japanese, and Korean language materials in all fields, but with an emphasis on the humanities and social sciences. The holdings of the East Asian collections reflect the interests of the faculty. Specific strengths are in materials on Chinese politics of the early 1950s, Chinese education, Japanese socialism, and Japanese literature of the Taisho and early Showa periods. The Library has recently begun to collect assertively in all areas of modern Korean studies, and particularly in materials relating to Korean communities outside of the Korean peninsula.

East Asian materials in other collections:

The Law Library collects books and other materials relevant to the study of law and legal practices in China and Japan.

Access:

The library is open to the public. Borrowing privileges are restricted to USC faculty, students, staff, and other members of the USC community, and to visiting scholars from RLG institutions. Non-USC borrowing privileges are available at a cost.

Interlibrary loan service:

Available to all libraries.

Online cataloging:

East Asian materials are cataloged in the OCLC CJK system.

Catalogs for use of the Collection:

Card Catalogs: East Asian card catalogs are maintained.

Online Catalog: The local online catalog, HOMER, includes romanized records for East Asian materials cataloged since 1988.

Network/Consortium affiliation:

Member of RLG and OCLC.

49. UNIVERSITY OF TEXAS, AUSTIN

East Asian Collection, The General Libraries
Austin, Texas 78712
Tel: (512) 495-4323

Kevin F. Lin, East Asian Librarian

Year started: 1958

Hours:

Weekdays: 8:00 am - 10 pm
Saturday: 9:00 am - 10 pm
Sunday: Noon - 10 pm

Holdings:

Volume:
    Chinese: 33,211
    Japanese: 42,524
Current serials:
    Chinese: 229
    Japanese: 207
Current newspapers:
    Chinese: 5
    Japanese: 3
Chinese and Japanese microfilm reels and fiche cards: 1,233

Areas of strength:

The collection holds materials primarily in Chinese and Japanese humanities and social sciences. Strong areas are:

Chinese: Modern literature and history (from the late Ch'ing period), language, philosophy, and politics.

Japanese: Modern literature and history (from the Meiji period), language, philosophy, business, economics, and politics.

East Asian materials in other collections:

The Fine Arts, Architecture, and Life Science Libraries have some holdings in the East Asian languages.

Access:

The library is open to the public. Borrowing privileges are extended to UT faculty, students, visiting scholars, faculty of other universities with which the General Libraries may establish lending agreements, Texas residents, etc.

Interlibrary loan service:

Available to all libraries.

Online cataloging:

East Asian materials are cataloged in the OCLC CJK system.

Catalogs for use of the Collection:

Card Catalogs: East Asian card catalogs are maintained.

Online Catalog: The local online catalog, UTCAT, includes records for CJK materials in romanized form only.

Network/Consortium affiliation:

Member of OCLC and AMIGOS Bibliographic Council, Inc.

50. UNIVERSITY OF TORONTO

Cheng Yu-Tung East Asian Library
130 St. George Street, 8th Floor
Toronto, Ontario, CANADA M5S 1A5
Tel: (416) 978-3300

Anna T. Liang U, East Asian Librarian

Year started: 1964

Hours:

Monday-Thursday: 9:00 am - 7:30 pm
Friday: 9:00 am - 6:00 pm
Saturday: Noon - 5:00 pm
Summer:
Monday-Thursday: 9:00 am - 7:00 pm
Friday: 9:00 am - 6:00 pm

Holdings:

Volume:
Chinese:	109,186
Japanese:	107,398
Korean:	4,144

Current serials:
Chinese:	305
Japanese:	165
Korean:	14

Current newspapers:
Chinese:	16
Japanese:	6

Chinese and Japanese microfilm reels and fiche cards: 9,129

Areas of strength:

The collection is primarily in Chinese, Japanese and Korean languages, with some western language reference titles, and covers the humanities, social and political sciences. Specific strengths lie in Chinese classics, traditional Chinese literature, Chinese local gazetteers, and modern Japanese literature.

Special collections:

The H.H. Mu Collection, which the library acquired in 1933 from Chinese scholar Mu Hsueh-hsun in Peking, contains some 40,000 volumes of scholarly works, including about 5,000 volumes of Chinese rare books and manuscripts on history, literature, and military science.

Access:

The library is open to the public. Borrowing privileges are given to faculty, students, and staff of the Ontario Universities members. Outside scholars and researchers may apply for research readers cards for checking out materials from the library.

Interlibrary loan service:

Available to all libraries.

Online cataloging:

East Asian materials are cataloged in the RLIN CJK system.

Catalogs for use of the Collection:

Card Catalogs: East Asian card catalogs are maintained but closed since December 17, 1990.

Online Catalog: The local online catalog is UTLAS which includes East Asian records in romanization only.

Network/Consortium affiliation:

Member of UTLAS and Associate Member of RLIN for its CJK program.

51. UNIVERSITY OF VIRGINIA

East Asia Collection, Alderman Library
Charlottesville, Virginia 22901
Tel: (804) 924-4978. FAX: (804) 924-4337.

Chung-ming Lung, East Asia Bibliographer

Year started: 1950

Hours:

Monday-Thursday: 8:00 am - Midnight
Friday: 8:00 am - 6:00 pm
Saturday: 9:00 am - 6:00 pm
Sunday: Noon - Midnight

Holdings:

Volume:
Chinese:	23,580
Japanese:	5,592
Korean:	280

Current serials:
Chinese:	88
Japanese:	60

Current newspapers:
Chinese:	7
Japanese:	2
East Asian microfilm reels and fiche cards:	529

Areas of strength:

The collection covers East Asian materials in almost all subject areas, with special emphases on Chinese modern history, Chinese student movements, materials on Chinese ethnic studies of the southwestern provinces, Buddhism, Japanese business history, and Japanese modern literature.

Special collections:

The Ma Kiam collection, acquired in 1965 from the later Prof. Ma Kiam of the University of Hong Kong, has about 15,000 volumes of Chinese collectanea and some individual works on Sinology.

Access:

The library is open to the public. Borrowing privileges are extended to all residents of Virginia and visiting scholars and research fellows at the University.

Interlibrary loan service:

Available to all libraries.

Online cataloging:

East Asian materials are cataloged in the OCLC CJK system.

Catalogs for use of the Collection:

Card Catalogs: East Asian card catalogs are maintained.

Online Catalog: The local online catalog, VIRGO, contains romanized records for all new East Asian titles catalogued since September 1989.

Network/Consortium affiliation:

Member of OCLC and SOLINET.

52. WASHINGTON UNIVERSITY, ST. LOUIS

East Asian Library, One Brookings Drive
St. Louis, Missouri 63130
Tel: (314) 889-5155. FAX: (314) 889-4719.

Sachiko Morrell, East Asian Librarian

Year started: 1964

Hours:

Weekdays: 8:30 am - 10:00 pm
Weekends: 1:00 pm - 6:00 pm
Summer and intersessions: 8:30 am - 5:00 pm (weekdays)

Holdings:

Volume:
Chinese:	62,537
Japanese:	41,610

Current serials:
Chinese:	230
Japanese:	170
Korean:	2

Current newspapers:
Chinese:	10
Japanese:	2
Korean:	1
Chinese microfilm reels and fiche cards:	1,308

Areas of strength:

The collection consists almost entirely of materials in Chinese and Japanese and covers all major subjects in the humanities and social sciences. Special strengths are in the fields of languages, literature, history, philosophy, religion, and art history.

Special collections:

The Robert Elegant Collection consists of four file cabinets containing news releases, newspaper clippings, and broad cast memos from mainland China gathered in Hong Kong during the Chinese Cultural Revolution, 1967-1976.

East Asian materials in other collections:

The Art Library has 1,200 volumes in Chinese/Japanese art and art history, and the Law Library has 900 volumes in Chinese law.

Access:

The library is open to the public. Borrowing privileges are given to faculty and students of the Washington University and other higher educational institutions in the metropolitan St. Louis area which have cooperative arrangements with the university, members of the Book Mark Society, and others under special arrangements.

Interlibrary loan service:

Available to all libraries.

Online Cataloging:

East Asian materials are cataloged in the OCLC CJK system.

Catalogs for use of the Collection:

Card Catalogs: East Asian card catalogs are maintained.

Online Catalog: The local online catalog, LUIS, has romanized records for East Asian materials with basic bibliographic information.

Network/Consortium affiliation:

Member of OCLC, NOTIS, the Midwest East Asian Library Group, and MLINC (the Missouri Library Network Corporation, or the Missouri Link).

Publications:

1. *Guide to Library Resources for Chinese Studies* (1978).

2. *Guide to Library Resources for Japanese Studies* (1987).

53. UNIVERSITY OF WASHINGTON

East Asia Library, Gowen Hall DO-27
Seattle, Washington 98195
Tel: (206) 543-4490. FAX: (206) 545-8049.

Min-chih Chou, Head

Year founded: 1937

Hours:

Monday-Thursday: 8:00 am - 5:00 pm; 7:00 pm - 10:00 pm
Friday: 8:00 am - 5:00 pm
Saturday: Noon - 4:00 pm
Summer and intersessions:
Monday-Friday: 8:00 am - 5:00 pm
Saturday: Noon - 4:00 pm

Holdings:

Volume:

Chinese:	186,855
Japanese:	96,557
Korean:	42,400

Current serials:

Chinese:	1,370
Japanese:	906
Korean:	587

Current newspapers:

Chinese:	49
Japanese:	10
Korean:	19

East Asian microfilm reels and fiche cards: 12,879

Areas of strength:

The library holds 345,700 volumes of printed materials, 11,055 reels of microfilm and 6,700 microfiches in Chinese, Japanese, Korean, Tibetan, Manchu, Mongolian, and western language publications of East Asia.

The Chinese Collection, the largest in the library, started in 1937 with a Rockefeller Grant purchase of Chinese literature. With the establishment of the Far Eastern Institute in 1946, and grants from the Ford and Mellon foundations, and the US Office of Education, this collection grew rapidly from the 1950s on, and has been enriched by the acquisition of the Joseph Rock Collection of gazetteers of Southwest China, the Hellmut Wilhelm collection of Chinese classics, the Ch'en Fan collection of 7,000 volumes (translations, modern Chinese literary works, and some Ch'ing dynasty essays) together with the Universal Book Company warehouse collection of the 1950-1970s publications.

The small Japanese collection was first augmented by the acquisition of the George Kerr Collection in 1948. The Robert Paine Collection of Japanese art materials purchased in 1968 greatly enhanced the Japanese holdings. Since 1986, emphasis has been placed on the Japanese political economy, due to an acquisition grant agreement with the Japan-US Friendship Commission. Substantial works on Japanese art history have been acquired since 1989, and a conscious effort has been made to acquire literary works on the aftermath of the atomic bombing of Japan, and primary resources on the study of Japanese women.

The Korean collection was established from the outgrowth of the Army Specialized Training Program for Korean language instruction during World War II. It has developed over the years into one of the largest in the nation, with emphases on language and literature, history, political science, and anthropology. Current acquisition effort has been focused onto building a collection of modern Korean poetry.

Special collections:

Chinese: *Mu-yu-shu* folk literature; Wu Hsien-tzu manuscript; Tiao-yu-tai collection; Canton Delta Collection; Ch'en Fan (former Chief editor of Ta Kung Pao in Hong Kong) Collection; Twenty-five Dynastic Histories Full Text Database; Chinese gazetteers, especially on the Southwest region in China, of the Rock Collection; and Union Research Institute newspaper clippings (1949-1970) on microfilm.

Japanese: Robert Paine Collection on Japanese painting; materials on left-wing activities in Japan during the period of 1920-1940; mimeographed records of the Tokyo War Crimes Trials donated by Dr. Robert Butow, an active participant in the trials.

East Asian materials in other collections:

The Marion G. Gallagher Law Library contains a substantial and regionally significant collection of foreign law with special emphasis on Chinese, Japanese, and Korean materials.

Access:

The general stacks of the library is open to the public. Periodicals has an "open stacks" policy for university users only (with occasional exceptions). Borrowing privileges are given to university faculty, students, staff, and anyone with a borrower's library card which is issued by the main library's Circulation Division. An application for the library card may be submitted by an individual or an organization.

Travel grants:

A travel grant of up to $600 may be obtained from the East Asian Center, Jackson School of International Studies, for use of the 25 Dynastic Histories database in the East Asia Library.

Interlibrary loan service:

Available to all libraries.

Online Cataloging:

East Asian materials are cataloged in the OCLC CJK system.

Catalogs for use of the Collection:

Card Catalogs: East Asian card catalogs are maintained.

Online Catalog: Approximately eight percent of the East Asia Library collection is accessible online through the local online catalog, GEAC, which contains East Asian records in romanization.

Network/Consortium affiliation:

Member of OCLC.

Publications:

1. *The Far Eastern Library of the University of Washington.* 1959.

2. *A Catalog of the Official Gazetteers of China in the University of Washington.* 1966.

3. *A Descriptive Catalog of the Ming Editions in the Far Eastern Library.* 1975.

4. *People's Republic of China: a Bibliography of Research and Primary Sources in English.* 1979.

5. *Japanese Economy and Politics: Selected Serial Titles in Japanese and English.* 1980

6. *University of Washington Libraries, East Asia Serials Catalog.* 1981.

7. *Current Chinese Serials in East Asia Library.* 1982.

8. *Current Japanese Serials in East Asia Library.* 1987.

9. *Current Korean Serial List in the East Asia Library at the University of Washington.* 1987.

10. *East Asia Library 1990 Yearbooks on China.* 1990.

11. *Union List of Current Japanese Serials in Six East Asian Libraries of Western North America* (British Columbia, U.C.-Berkeley, UCLA, Hawaii, Hoover, and Washington), compiled by Mihoko Miki. [Los Angeles]: Western Regional Japanese Library Conference, 1988.

54. UNIVERSITY OF WISCONSIN

East Asian Collection, Memorial Library
728 State Street, Madison, Wisconsin 53706
Tel: (608) 262-0344. FAX: (608) 263-3684.

Chester Wang, East Asian Bibliographer

Year started: 1964

Hours:

Monday-Thursday: 8:00 am - 11:45 pm
Friday: 8:00 am - 9:45 pm
Saturday: 10:00 am - 9:45 pm
Sunday: 10:00 am - 11:45 pm
Intersessions:
Monday-Friday: 8:00 am - 9:45 pm
Saturday and Sunday: 10:00 am - 9:45 pm

Holdings:

Volumes:
Chinese:	89,759
Japanese:	49,780
Korean:	1,534

Current serials:
Chinese:	301
Japanese:	172
Korean:	14

Current newspapers:
Chinese:	4
Japanese:	2
Korean:	2

Areas of strength:

The collection is strong in the humanities and social sciences. Specific strengths lie in language, literature, history, philosophy, religion (Buddhism), fine arts, sociology, economics, politics and government, and reference works. The library's Buddhist collection is one of the best in American libraries.

East Asian materials in other collections:

The Art and Music Libraries house East Asian materials on these subjects.

Access:

The library is open to the public. A currently valid ID is required to enter the library. Borrowing privileges are given to faculty, students, and staff of the UW system; faculty spouses and children; Wisconsin state employees; faculty from CIC member institutions; and others with a currently valid Memorial Library card, which may be obtained at the Memorial Library Card Application Window by the library's entrance.

Interlibrary loan service:

Available to all libraries.

Online Cataloging:

East Asian materials are cataloged in the RLIN CJK system.

Catalogs for use of the Collection:

Card Catalogs: East Asian card catalogs are maintained.

Online Catalog: The local online catalog, NLS (Network Library System), contains some East Asian records in romanization.

Network/Consortium affiliation:

Member of OCLC and CIC.

55. YALE UNIVERSITY

East Asian Collection, 120 High Street
New Haven, Connecticut 06520
Tel: (203) 432-1790. FAX: (203) 432-7231.

Hideo Kaneko, Curator

Year started: 1878

Hours:

Monday-Thursday: 8:30 am - 10:00 pm
Friday: 8:30 am - 5:00 pm
Saturday: 10:00 am - 5:00 pm
Sunday: 1:00 pm - 10:00 pm

Holdings:

Volume:
Chinese:	317,502
Japanese:	173,514
Korean:	6,095

Current serials:
Chinese:	1,202
Japanese:	1,139
Korean:	36

Current newspapers:
Chinese:	27
Japanese:	4
Korean:	3

East Asian microfilm reels and fiche cards: 5,886

Areas of strength:

The collection represents one of the largest holdings in East Asian humanities and social sciences in American libraries. The Chinese collection is especially strong in the traditional fields of Sinology: history, language, literature, classics, and philosophy. It has unusual strength in the history of institutions and of Buddhism in China. The general field of Chinese literature is well represented, and the Yale University Library probably has the best collection of modern literature since 1919 in the country. There is a good history of art collection, and strong archaeology and modern history collections. More recent emphasis has been put on strengthening social sciences holdings, and the collection today is quite strong in social sciences, especially in Chinese law and economics. Furthermore, the Yale collection of current and recent Chinese periodicals is one of the best in the nation.

The Japanese collection is especially strong in the traditional fields of Japanology: history, language, literature, art, and thought. Outside of Japan, it probably has the best accumulation of materials relating to institutional development, particularly of the late feudal period. It is very strong in language and linguistics and getting stronger in literature in recent years. Another field expanded in recent years is Buddhism. The Japanese Collection is also strong in the social sciences.

Korean language holdings are limited and are strongest in language and linguistics. Current emphasis of acquisitions has been to build a collection of basic Korean reference works, materials relevant to the study of the language, and some historical source materials.

Special collections:

Japanese Manuscript Collection: Some 700 titles in 1,200 volumes of Japanese manuscripts and codices in history, literature, economics, etc., dated 17th century through early 20th century. Most of these were acquired in 1906-07.

Yale Association of Japan Collection: Some 350 items of manuscripts, codices, books, and objects to illustrate Japanese civilization, dated 8th century through 20th century--a donation by the Yale Association of Japan in 1934.

The Jen Yu-wen Collection on the Taiping Revolutionary Movement: The Jen Yu-wen Collection comprises materials which the donor, a noted scholar on the Taiping Movement of 1851 to 1866, spent more than a half century gathering. The Collection contains some 463 volumes of bound materials which range from ordinary but necessary printed books, through very rare items, to some manuscripts, original Taiping documents and Taiping related letters, seven large rubbings of Taiping monuments, 128 genuine and spurious Taiping coins, four wooden seals of Taiping officers, one brass identification tag for Taiping soldiers, and miscellaneous materials on the Taiping Movement.

The Tibetan Collection, one of the most important Tibetan collections in North America, includes 600 volumes of texts printed in Tibet (inclusive of a complete set of the Lhasa edition of Kanjur), 350 volumes of non-Tibetan imprints (in English and various foreign languages on Tibet as well as Tibetan texts printed outside of Tibet), over 4,000 volumes of Tibetan materials, 6 manuscript texts, 9 manuscript fragments of texts, 49 tankas, 123 iconographical prints, and 22 objects (statues, beads, prayer wheels, bells, drums, etc.).

East Asian materials in other collections:

The Japanese Manuscript Collection, the Yale Association of Japan Collection, and the Tibetan Collection (described above) are in the Beinecke Rare Book and Manuscript Library.

Access:

The library is open to the public with restrictions. Stack and borrowing privileges are extended to Yale faculty, students, and staff. Others may be granted such privileges with approval and upon payment of a fee. East Asian scholars in Southern New England may receive free stack access through a special program (contact the Curator of the East Asian Collection).

Interlibrary loan service:

Available to all libraries.

Online cataloging:

East Asian materials are cataloged in the RLIN CJK system.

Catalogs for use of the Collection:

Card Catalogs: East Asian card catalogs are maintained.

Online Catalog: The local online catalog, ORBIS (Online Research and Bibliographic Information System), has all the East Asian records the library input into RLIN since 1983. ORBIS CJK records are available in romanized form only. As of January 31, 1991, there were 69,104 CJK records in the online catalog, about 26% of the total CJK titles at Yale.

Network/Consortium affiliation:

Member of RLG and the East Coast East Asian Library Consortium.

Publications:

1. Kaneko, Hideo. "Japanese Heritage: An Exhibition of the Yale Association of Japan Collection," *CEAL Newsletter* no. 43 (March 1974): 13-15.

2. _____. "Kan'ichi Asakawa and the Yale University Library," *CEAL Bulletin* no. 75 (October 1984): 22-32.

3. Suddard, Adrienne. "Jen Yu-wen Collection on the Taiping Revolutionary Movement," *Yale University Library Gazette* v. 49, no. 3 (January 1975): 293-296.

4. *Union List of Japanese Periodicals in the East Asian Libraries of Columbia, Harvard, Princeton, and Yale Universities*, second edition, 1989; bilingual.

List of Collections
by Geographical Distribution

(References are to entry numbers of collections)

East

Brown University: East Asian Collection, 5
Columbia University: C.V. Starr East Asian Library, 16
Cornell University: Wason Collection, 17
Dartmouth College: Oriental Collection, 18
Free Gallery of Art/Arthur M. Sackler Gallery: Library, 22
Georgetown University: East Asian Collection, 23
Harvard University: Harvard-Yenching Library, 24
Institute for Advanced Studies of World Religions: The Library, 29
Library of Congress: Asian Division, 32
Library of Congress: Far Eastern Law Division, 33
University of Maryland: East Asia Collection, 34
New York Public Library: Oriental Division, 37
University of Pennsylvania: East Asia Collection, 42
University of Pittsburgh: East Asian Library, 43
Princeton University: Gest Oriental Library and East Asian Collections 44
University of Rochester: Asia Library, 45
Rutgers State University: East Asian Library, 47
University of Virginia: East Asia Collection, 51
Yale University: East Asian Collection, 55

Midwest

Center for Research Libraries, 12
University of Chicago: East Asian Library, 13
Far Eastern Research Library, 21
University of Illinois: Asian Library, 27
Indiana University: East Asian Collection, 28
University of Iowa: Oriental Collection, 30
University of Kansas: East Asian Library, 31
University of Michigan: Asia Library, 35
University of Minnesota: East Asian Library, 36
Oberlin College: East Asian Collection, 39
Ohio State University: East Asian Collection, 40
Washington University: East Asian Library, 52
University of Wisconsin: East Asian Collection, 54

Mountain

University of Arizona: Oriental Studies Collection, 1
Arizona State University: East Asian Language Collection, 2
Brigham Young University: Asian Collection, 3
University of Colorado, Boulder: East Asiatic Library, 15
Family History Library: Asian Collection, 20

South

Duke University: East Asian Collection, 19
University of North Carolina: East Asian Collection, 38
University of Texas, Austin: East Asian Collection, 49

West and Hawaii

University of California, Berkeley: East Asian Library, 6
University of California, Davis: Asian Languages Collection, 7
University of California, Irvine: East Asian Collection, 8
University of California, Los Angeles: Richard C. Rudolph East Asian
   Library, 9
University of California, San Diego: International Relations and Pacific
   Studies Library, 10
University of California, Santa Barbara: East Asian Studies Collection, 11

Claremont Colleges: Asian Studies Collection, 14
University of Hawaii, Manoa: Asia Collection, 25
Hoover Institution: East Asian Collection, 26
University of Oregon: Orientalia Collection, 41
University of Southern California: East Asian Library, 48
University of Washington: East Asia Library, 53

Canada

University of British Columbia: Asian Studies Library, 4
Royal Ontario Museum: H.H. Mu Library, 46
University of Toronto: Cheng Yu-Tung East Asian Library, 50

Index

(References are to entry numbers of collections)

About the Compiler

THOMAS H. LEE is East Asian Librarian at the Indiana University Library.
His most recent book is AACR 2 Workbook for East Asian Publications (1983).

www.ingramcontent.com/pod-product-compliance
Lightning Source LLC
Chambersburg PA
CBHW070443100426
42812CB00004B/1195